Edward Caird

The Social Philosophy and Religion of Comte

Edward Caird

The Social Philosophy and Religion of Comte

ISBN/EAN: 9783337077532

Printed in Europe, USA, Canada, Australia, Japan

Cover: Foto ©Thomas Meinert / pixelio.de

More available books at **www.hansebooks.com**

THE SOCIAL PHILOSOPHY AND RELIGION OF COMTE.

BY

EDWARD CAIRD, LL.D.,

PROFESSOR OF MORAL PHILOSOPHY IN THE UNIVERSITY OF GLASGOW.

GLASGOW

JAMES MACLEHOSE & SONS,

Publishers to the University.

1885.

Dedicated,

To

MY FRIEND AND COLLEAGUE

JOHN NICHOL.

b

CONTENTS.

CHAPTER III.

THE POSITIVE OR CONSTRUCTIVE SIDE OF COMTE'S PHILOSOPHY
—HIS SUBSTITUTES FOR METAPHYSIC AND THEOLOGY.

CHAPTER IV.

COMTE'S VIEW OF THE RELATION OF THE INTELLECT TO THE
HEART—ITS EFFECT ON HIS CONCEPTION OF HISTORY AND
OF THE SOCIAL IDEAL.

PREFACE.

THIS volume consists of a series of articles which have already appeared in the *Contemporary Review*, and which the proprietors of that review have kindly permitted me to republish. A few paragraphs have been re-written, and a few verbal changes introduced to remove obscurity or inaccuracy, but the general substance of the articles remains unaltered.

In the following exposition and criticism of Comte's philosophy I have considered it mainly, though not exclusively, in its ethical and religious aspects. I have not attempted to deal with the detailed discussion of the nature and methods of the sciences contained in the *Philosophie Positive*, except in so far as is necessary for the understanding of the *Politique Positive*, in which

the social and religious aims of Comte's philosophy
are for the first time explicitly stated. Not,
indeed, that there is any very marked division
between his earlier and his later treatises. The
changes observable in the latter do not amount,
as has sometimes been represented, to a sudden
revolution, but are rather the last development
of tendencies which had been gaining ground in
Comte's mind as his work advanced, and gradually
carrying him away from his original principles,
or at least greatly modifying their first significance. I have preferred, however, to confine
myself, in the main, to the social philosophy of
Comte and the restoration of religion connected
therewith, partly because I have not sufficient
scientific knowledge to estimate the value of his
critical review of mathematics and physics,
chemistry and biology, and partly because, so
far as I know, there has been very little serious
criticism of that part of his work which he
regarded (I think justly) as the most important
and original. In his earlier treatise, or at least
in the greater part of it, Comte was working
upon lines which are common to him with all
the representatives of what in the last century

was termed "Enlightenment," and now most often goes by the names of "Positivism" or "Agnosticism." But the distinctive peculiarity of Comte is that he does not stop at that negation of metaphysics and theology which is characteristic of this school, but that *his* Positivism reproduces both, though in a new form. It is, indeed, just this new element in Comte which gives a truly "positive" meaning to his well-known law of development, which in its first form might more truly be described as "negative." For in that form all that it distinctly tells us about the development of the human mind is that man once believed in theological or metaphysical fictions, and that he has now ceased, or is gradually ceasing, to believe in them. In his later writings, however, Comte has come to see that both theology and metaphysics are based upon perennial wants of man's spiritual nature, wants which, as man, he cannot but feel, and for which a real and not merely a fictitious satisfaction can be provided. He teaches us, therefore, to regard the progress of man as a true development, in which the passing away of the first forms of his higher life is incidental to the further manifestation of the spirit, which was once expressed in them. Hence the last or "positive" stage of thought is conceived to be a negation and abolition of the past in which all that gave the past its value is reaffirmed and maintained. It is a higher "positive," which is reached through the negation of the lower, but it is itself a great deal more than that negation.

Now, the ultimate interest of Comte's philosophy lies in the success or failure of this attempt of his to find a new satisfaction for those higher wants of humanity, which Theology and Metaphysic, or, as I should prefer to say, Religion and Philosophy, have so long been supposed to satisfy. It is not difficult to describe, at least in general terms, what these wants are. Philosophy professes to seek and to find the principle of unity which underlies all the manifold particular truths of the separate sciences, and in reference to which they can be brought together and organized as a system of knowledge. And Religion, while it also is concerned with an absolute principle of reality, differs from Philosophy mainly in this, that it is not merely or primarily theoretical. For Religion what is required is such a conviction as to the ultimate basis of our existence as shall enable us to find therein at once an adequate object of affection and a sufficient aim for all our practical endeavours. Now a scientific Agnosticism, such as is common at the present day, means either that there are no such wants in man, or that, if they exist, no provision is made for their satisfaction. Such an Agnosticism could scarcely find a better expression for itself than the Comtean law of intellectual development; for, as that law is commonly understood, it implies that the whole progress of man has been just his gradual awakening to the necessity of renouncing all effort to penetrate to the reality which is hidden behind the veil of phenomena. On this view, it is vain for man to ask any longer the question of Philosophy, or to attempt to find a support for his life in the faiths and hopes of religion. Man is but a link or a series of links in the endless chain of phenomenal causes; his utmost knowledge cannot reach beyond the relations of particular things to each other and to his own particular existence, and whatever he may desire, to these relations he must be content practically to limit himself. *Tecum habita et noris quam sit tibi curta supellex.*

Now the peculiarity of **Comte's** position is that he admits the principle on which this Agnostic view is based, and yet at the same time rejects the conclusions which are usually and naturally drawn from it. He accepts the situation as he understands it. He admits and contends that Philosophy is defeated in its attempt to reach an absolute principle—a principle of unity, which is at once the real or objective centre of the universe, and the subjective centre for our knowledge of it. He admits and contends that there is a great gulf fixed between the absolute reality of things and our consciousness of them. Nevertheless, he holds that, in a sense, we may still aspire to that encyclopædic or universal view of things which Philosophy pretended to give; for, though we cannot reach an objective principle of unity in things, we can still gather knowledge to a subjective centre, by regarding all things in relation to our own needs and uses. This, however, does not mean that we are to view everything in relation to our own individual pleasures and pains. For the individual is essentially related to his race, or rather, as we should say, that the "individual man is a mere abstraction, and that there is nothing real but Humanity." Hence, in knowledge and in feeling we are carried beyond ourselves; and as in our moral life we can rise from egoism to altruism, so in our intellectual life we can learn to regard the world from the point of view, not of the individual, but of the race. And the same change brings with it the restoration of religion. The "objective" or absolute God, the God who made all things work together for good to His creatures, has disappeared with the fictions of childhood. But His place has been taken by Humanity, conceived as a great providential existence, which sustains and controls the life of the individual man, and in which he finds a sufficient object for all his devotion. Looking to this Great Being, man need not feel the want of any other God. He has before his eyes One who can help him and whom he can love and serve. Or if he should still feel something wanting, as an object of worship, in a Being who is not the Absolute Being, he is at liberty to indulge in the poetic illusion which makes

Nature, as well as Humanity, the friend of man. If he does so, however, he must remember that he *is* yielding to an illusion, which is not supported by anything we know of Nature; for Nature, apart from the action of man upon it, shows itself as a mere fatality, which is altogether indifferent to his weal or woe.

Even this short sketch of Comte's system—for the detailed exposition of which the reader is referred to the following chapters—may suffice to show where the vital spot, the Achilles' heel, of Comte's philosophy lies. It lies in the idea of a " subjective synthesis " or relative centre of knowledge. This idea for Comtists is the *articulus stantis vel cadentis philosophiae.* If this central principle can be securely defended, it matters little to the orthodox Positivist how many of the subordinate elements of Comte's thought may have to be abandoned or modified. If it has to be surrendered, however numerous and valuable may be the separate truths and suggestions which are discoverable in every part of Comte's works, his philosophy as a whole must be given up. From what I have read of the works of Comte's most zealous and discerning followers, I am disposed to think that they would be ready to accept this issue.   Now Comte's position has generally been attacked, if one might so express it, from the rear, *i.e.*, by those whose views accord most with his earlier doctrine expressed in the *Philosophie Positive*, and who regard him as abandoning the true Positivism when he admits any philosophical or religious synthesis whatever, whether subjective or objective, whether relative or absolute.   It is in this way that Comte was assailed by Littré, the most eminent of his French disciples, and it is in this way also that he was criticised by Mill and Lewes, who, without being strictly his disciples, accepted most of the leading ideas of his earlier work.   If there is any novelty in the criticism contained in the following pages, it is that it starts from the opposite point of view, and seeks to show that the true synthesis of philosophy must be objective as well as subjective, and that there can be no religion of Humanity which is not also a religion of God.   And this means that it is logically impossible to go beyond the merely individualistic point of view with which Comte started, except on the assumption that the intelligence of man is, or involves, a universal principle of knowledge. The same arguments, in fact, which break down the division between man and man, break down also the division between man and nature; for, if all Humanity be considered as organically united, it becomes impossible not to recognize in nature an essential relation to man, which makes it in some sense a part of the same organism. The history of the development of Comte's thought is itself, as I endeavour in the sequel to show, an evidence of this principle: for it is the history of a development which ends by all but retracting the negations with which it begins. And when, in his *Synthèse Subjective,* Comte sanctions the poetic treatment of Space and the Earth as divine friends of man, and members of a kind of Trinity in which Humanity is the third person, he comes very near to a complete return upon himself. It has, indeed, been contended by Dr. Bridges* that this is but the ordinary license of poetry, such, for instance, as we find in Shelley's Earth-hymn in the "Prometheus Unbound." "Supposing any one had taken Shelley seriously to task for maintaining that the Earth is alive, should

* Unity of Comte's Life and Doctrine, p. 60.

we not think him curiously dull and pedantic?"
True, it may be answered: but, supposing any
one had maintained that the earth is not *in any
sense* the expression of that spiritual principle
which expresses itself in a higher way in living
beings, and above all in man, and that, therefore,
there is nothing *but* fiction in the ascription of
life to it, should we not be entitled to say that
he had lost hold of the sense in which poetry is
truth? Should we not consider that he had
degraded poetry from a sensuous and therefore
partly fictitious presentment of ideal truth, into a
mere plaything of fancy which bodies forth things
that are not as if they were? In Comte's case
the interest of the poetic fiction consists in this,
that it was the imaginative anticipation of a truth
towards which he was moving, but which he
had not distinctly recognized. His imagination
had already emancipated him from the limits
of those earlier opinions of his, which still held
good for his understanding. If he had taken
one step farther, the wheel would have "come
full circle," and he would have restored both
Theology and Philosophy to the place from
which he expelled them. He would have

"burnt what he had adored, and adored what he had burnt."

I cannot say so much in criticism of Comte's views without adding—what every new reading of his works, and especially of the *Politique Positive* makes me feel more strongly—that the value of his teaching is by no means to be estimated by its mere logical result. Whatever may be said of his philosophy as a whole, he possessed that unmistakeable instinct for truth which renders even the errors and inconsistencies of men of genius more instructive than the most unexceptionable reasonings of many judicious persons, who follow the beaten tracks of thought and, therefore, "need no repentance."

ERRATUM.—Page 56, Contents, 6th line, for *Religion* read *Realism.*

THE SOCIAL PHILOSOPHY AND RELIGION
OF COMTE.

CHAPTER I.

GENERAL ACCOUNT OF COMTE'S PHILOSOPHY.

Comte's fundamental principles—Their bearing on his view of history—Decay of theology and of the social system founded on it—Metaphysic, its strength for destruction and weakness for construction—It prepares the way for positive science, on which the social system of the future must be based—Necessity for a new religion based on science—Humanity the true object of worship—The social system corresponding to the religion of Humanity—Man's intellectual and moral powers evolved in conflict with nature—The nature of the social organization and the three forms of society, the Family, the State, and the Church—The Priesthood of Humanity and its office.

IT is impossible to understand the errors of a great writer unless we do justice to the truth which underlies them. In judging of Comte's philosophy, and especially of his social philosophy, this law of criticism has often been neglected, even by those who, from their general philosophical point of view, might seem best qualified to

A

appreciate him.   Disagreeing as I do with many
of his conclusions, I cannot hope to be entirely
successful in doing him justice.   But the attempt
to do so may have its use, if only in bringing to
light the relationship of philosophies which are
commonly regarded as having no connection with
each other.   The spirit of the time is greater than
any of its expressions, and it moulds them all,
under whatever outward diversity of form, to a
common result.   If there is anything which the
history of philosophy teaches with clearness, it is
that contemporaneous movements of the human
spirit, even those which appear to be most independent or antagonistic, are but partial expressions
of a truth which is not fully revealed in any one
of them, and which can be adequately appreciated
only by a later generation.   The present is said
to be *par excellence* the age of historical criticism ;
but the historical imagination is worth little if it
does not enable us to discover identity of nature
under the most varied disguises, and, instead of
being confined to the formulæ of any one philosophy, to remould and renew our own ideas by
entering into the minds of others.   In order to
prepare the way for a just appreciation of the

teaching of Comte, I shall, in this chapter, give
a short sketch of his philosophy (and more
particularly of his social philosophy) as far as
possible from his own point of view, reserving
for subsequent chapters what I have to say
in the way of criticism.

There are two main thoughts which rule the
mind of Comte, and are the sources of most of
the peculiarities of his system. The one is, "the
law of the three stages"; the other is the subordination of science to man's social well-being,
or, as he expresses it, of the intellect to the
heart. The first of these thoughts embodies his
criterion of knowledge; the second is the principle by which he seeks to systematize knowledge,
and to estimate the relative value of its parts.
The relation of these two points in the mind
of Comte will be best understood if we recall his
historical position and the early course of his
mental development. As with most educated
Frenchmen of his time, Comte's first thoughts on
social politics were suggested by the Revolution;
and his youthful connection with St. Simon
showed that he shared in that reaction against
the individualistic philosophy of the Eighteenth

The two leading ideas in Comte.

Century, which gave rise to so many socialistic and communistic theories. In the school of St. Simon, Comte learned the falsehood of the gospel of Rousseau—that last quintessence of the philosophy which found reality only in the individual, and which, therefore, idealized the natural man as he is apart from, and prior to, all society, and regarded all social influence as deteriorating from his original purity. The hollowness of that theory had been written in letters of blood on the page of recent history, and that too plainly to be ignored by the most hopeful theorist on social subjects. Nor could any one who had read it there, fail to perceive also the less striking failure of the same doctrines in their economical form. The liberation of the individual had not brought to man political salvation, but had rather revealed his essential weakness when emancipated from the restraints of social order. "Laissez faire" had not, as was expected, introduced an economic millennium; but had rather given rise to a struggle of interests, which, if not moderated by any higher principle, might end in the dissolution of society. Hence the mere irrational movement of reaction drove the mass of men to bind again upon themselves the fetters which the Revolution had broken, and taught those who, like De Maistre, represented the ideas and interests of the past, the speculative strength of their position. De Maistre saw clearly that mere individualism is anarchy, and that the moral education of man is possible only through some binding social force. Nor was it difficult for a skilful special pleader like him to confound this truth with the doctrine that the only safety for civilization lay in a renewed submission to the mediæval order of Church and State. On the other hand, men who were too much imbued with the modern spirit to be moved by this reactionary logic, were led to detach the socialistic idea from the special form it had taken in past history, and to seek for some new form of political organization, in which individual freedom should be again subordinated to social order. Such men were St. Simon and Fourier—not, in any sense, great or comprehensive thinkers, but writers who were effective and influential for the moment simply because they represented the abstraction which was then rising into favour, and which had at least this to recommend it, that it was the opposite abstraction to that of the Revolutionists. Comte was too robust and manysided to remain long under the influence either of the concrete or of the abstract reactionaries—either of those who sought to return to the form, or of those who sought to return to the spirit, of the past. But his temporary subjection to St. Simon, and his ultimate revolt against him, help us in some measure to understand that double movement of thought out of which his system sprung. His subjection indicated that he had seen the insufficiency and unreality, the abstract and unhistorical character, of the gospel of mere rebellion. His emancipation from St. Simon indicated his discovery that the simple repression of rebellion, the mere closing up of the ranks of society under a social despotism, was an utterly inadequate solution of the difficulty. The problem before him, therefore, was to do justice to the element of truth in each of these movements—to the social impulse on the one hand and to the critical movement of intelligence on the other,—and to reconcile them in a higher unity. Socialism had taught him that social enthusiasm might be separated from the religious and political institutions on which it had rested in the past; and the progress of science seemed to teach him that intelligence has a constructive as well as a critical influence. The solution, therefore, was simply to take the former, as determining the end and goal of all practical effort; and the latter, as teaching us the proper means for its attainment. The enthusiasm of humanity guided by science, science directed so as to secure the highest happiness of humanity, were thus the two ideas by which the course of his thoughts was determined.

In the first place these ideas gave to Comte *Their bearing on his view of history* what seemed to him a perfect key to the history of the past. Man he conceives of as a being who at first is divided between weak social tendencies which bind him to his fellows, and strong selfish, or, as he calls them, *personal* instincts, which make him their rival and their enemy; yet without the triumph of the former over the latter there can be no security for his welfare or even for his existence. This triumph of social sympathy is the first necessity of civilization; and in an early age any theory of life must be welcome which promises to secure it.

The first social leaders of mankind, even if such
an idea could have presented itself to them,
could not wait with patience till experience had
revealed to them the true nature of man and the
world he lives in.   Their ignorance and their
benevolent haste to organize society, and to bind
men together in the bonds of a definite faith,
made them eagerly grasp at the first explanation
of the universe which imagination suggested;
and that first explanation was of course anthropomorphic.   "As they watched nature, as their
eyes wandered over the surface of the profound
ocean, instead of the bed hidden under the
waters, they saw nothing but the reflection of
their own faces."*   Hence the first moral order
and social discipline established among men was
based upon a theological explanation of the
universe.   Nor did the insecurity of the foundation seem for a long time to interfere with the
firmness of the superstructure.   The union of
men was like the union of an army—a union
of men bound together for life and death, though
the bond that united them was but a fairy tale.
Yet, in the long run, it was impossible that

* Turgot.

criticism should not make itself heard. Advancing experience, as it disclosed that the world is no plaything of arbitrary wills but an order of fixed law, gradually limited the free play of imagination, and removed the gods to a greater and greater distance. When, therefore, phenomena were seen to group themselves in large genera, with permanent attributes and relations, Polytheism rose out of Fetichism; and when the idea of the unity of the world, and of the general persistency of its laws, began to prevail, theology was inevitably reduced to the conception of one — overruling will which, directly or by its ministers, controls the whole movement of things. Up to this point the theological form of thought persisted: in one point of view it might even be said that, up to this point, it was strengthening its hold upon men. For, every successive concentration of the divine power made the idea of it a firmer and more comprehensive bond of social order, until at length the levelling and organizing genius of Rome laid the foundation of the universal empire, and Christian Monotheism broke down the walls of division between races and nations.

·But this apparent advance of the theological spirit was illusive, for it was really due to an intellectual movement, which must, in the long run, prove fatal to that spirit. The concentration of Fetichism into Polytheism, and of Polytheism into Monotheism, was really the gradual withdrawal of theology from the explanation of the universe, till, finally, it was driven to its last stronghold, its most general and abstract form. Hence the hour of its greatest social triumph was that which preceded its decisive fall. The same growing perception of the order of the world under general laws, which had forced the theologian first to substitute a limited for an indefinite number of divine wills, and then to substitute one will for this limited number, necessarily and inevitably awakened a doubt whether there is in nature any indication of will at all. Monotheism had represented the world as a general order of fixed laws, only interrupted by exceptional miracles; but increasing knowledge made miracles more and more incredible, till at last the theologians were reduced to the assertion that their God had once performed them, but that he performed them no longer. When this point was reached, it was not difficult to see that the whole anthropomorphic explanation of things was on the eve of disappearing. A God, who was nearer man in the past than he is in the present, could not be the God of the future.

But even before this period, the growing weakness of the theoretical basis of belief had begun to affect the practical life of men. The social order was built upon theology, and therefore the advance of the critical spirit was continually loosening its foundations. Hence the fierce hostility of the representatives of that order to the freedom of the intelligence. That hostility, however, is to be attributed not so much to their indignation at unbelief in itself, as to their alarm at the dissolution of social order which was its practical result. Nor was it altogether inexcusable, so long as the assailants of the old faith were unable to propound any theoretical principles which could be made the basis of reconstruction. Now the metaphysical principles to which these assailants appealed were really negations pretending to be affirmations, the purely negative character of which must reveal itself

And of the social order connected with it.

as soon as their victory was achieved. Men in whom the practical and organizing impulse was strong, who felt the necessity for a moral order, could not but see that such ropes of sand were no real substitute for the old framework of social and political life, and they were therefore tempted to shut their eyes to the intellectual claims of a truth which could be fertile only in destruction. Thus arose that fatal division between the heart and the intellect which has lasted down to the present day, and which must last till the intellect shows itself capable of producing a system which can more securely sustain the social order, and more completely satisfy the affections and spiritual aspirations of men, than the fictions of theology.

The metaphysical system of thought. The truth of this view will be more clearly seen if we examine the nature of that intermediate system of critical thought which was the great weapon of attack upon theology. This system was, in fact, only the last abstraction of the theological anthropomorphism itself. As in one department of human thought after another the knowledge of the uniform and unchangeable order of things prevailed over the conception of accident

and arbitrary change, the idea of will became
attenuated, until it ultimately disappeared altogether from the explanation of nature. But it
left behind a kind of spectre of abstraction.
Instead of being dominated by gods, phenomena
were supposed to be dominated by essences and
powers, which, however, were merely abstract
repetitions of those phenomena. How abstractions came to be thus substantiated as real
entities, separate from the phenomena in which
they were manifested, might be difficult to understand, if we did not remember that they were but
the residua of what had once been individualized
pictures of imagination. The essences of the
Schoolmen were but the dry bones of the living
creatures of poetry which the understanding had
slain. "The human mind," as Mill puts it, "did
not set out from the notion of a name, but from
that of a divinity. The realization of abstractions
was not the embodiment of a word, but the dis-
embodiment of a Fetich." Really, therefore, these
essences and powers were nothing more than the
pure abstractions, and therefore only the negations,
of the gods whose places they took. They had
no positive content of their own. As mere

negatives they had no value except in relation to the corresponding affirmatives, although in the first instance imagination was strong enough to give them the semblance of positive principles occupying the place of the beliefs they expelled. And it was just this temporary illusion which made them such powerful weapons of destruction. For the revolutionary passion can never be sustained by negations which it recognizes as such. It is impossible to march with enthusiasm to the attack upon the institutions of the past, without the conviction that there is something more to be gained than the destruction of those institutions.

Development of Metaphysic.

The metaphysical philosophy, as the necessary forerunner of the philosophy of experience, gradually extended its destructive power over all branches of human knowledge. At first it laid its hand on the sciences that deal with inorganic nature, and of these, first of all on those that deal with the phenomena furthest from man, and least subject to his control. For man discovers that the phenomena of the heavens are not ruled by arbitrary will, long before he discerns the absence of caprice from the general course of nature. In like manner, he is sensible that inorganic things have fixed and unchangeable relations, while as yet the spontaneity of animal life seems to be as unlimited as that which he attributes to his own will. And only last of all does it dawn upon him that his own life also is limited and controlled by something, which is neither his own will nor the will of a being like himself whom he can propitiate or persuade— something which is both within and without him, to which he must conform himself, seeing it will not conform to him. The last substantiated abstraction, therefore, which is put in the place of the divine powers, is Nature. And Nature is only a name for the general course of things, though it is regarded by metaphysics as existing apart from and controlling them. But as Nature succeeds to the place of a God whom men were conceived to be bound to obey, but able arbitrarily to disobey, so it is represented as the source of a law distinct from the actual course of human life, and to which it does not necessarily conform. The law of nature, in this view, is a law written on man's heart, but not necessarily realized in his actions. In truth, however, it is but the negation of that order of social life which was based upon the theological idea, though its negative character is necessarily hidden from those who believe in it.

Its power for de-struction. This becomes evident whenever we examine the main articles contained in this supposed law of nature. For these are simply negations of different parts of that social order which was based upon theology. The first of these articles is the right of private judgment—that is, the right of every individual to emancipate himself from all spiritual authority, and to judge of everything for himself. This principle is merely "a sanction of the state of anarchy, which intervened between the decay of the old discipline and the formation of new spiritual ties." In other words, it is not a new principle of order, but the abstract expression of the ungoverned state of mere individual opinion, "for no association whatever, even of the smallest number of persons and for the most temporary objects, can subsist without some degree of intellectual and moral agreement between its members." In the next place, among the articles of the law of nature, stands the doctrine of equality, which has a meaning only as the negation of the old hierarchy, the old social and political order, but which, taken absolutely, is the negation of all order whatever. For if society is anything more than a collection of unrelated atoms, if it is an organic unity, it must have different organs for its different functions; and it is as impossible that these organs should all be equal, as that they should all be the same. This doctrine, therefore, is but the abstract proclamation of social anarchy. To these articles are commonly added the doctrines of national independence, and of the sovereignty of the people. The former is nothing more than the negation of that spiritual supremacy of the Church, which in the Middle Ages mediated between the nations of Europe and made them one community; but, taken absolutely, it would imply national isolation and international anarchy. The latter is the transference to the governed of that fiction of divine right which was formerly supposed to reside in the governor, and it has no meaning except as the negation of that fiction. For the people cannot rule themselves; and even to make them choose their ruler, that is, to make the inferior and less wise choose the superior and wiser, cannot be regarded as more than a provisional expedient for anarchic times.

B

Its weakness for constrction.

The articles of the law of nature, then, like all metaphysical principles, are merely principles of insurrection and revolt. They have no positive validity ; for they are just the ultimate abstractions, or, so to speak, the speculative phantoms of the system which they destroy. As it is said that a man dies when he has seen his own ghost, so, according to Comte, the destroyer of theology is just the ghost of itself, raised by abstraction. But the ghost also vanishes when its victim is fairly buried, leaving the field to the growing strength of positive science.

It prepares the way for science

Positive science, then, is the real cause of all intellectual progress, its advance constitutes the *nisus formativus* that is concealed beneath the surface struggle of theology and metaphysics. For even in the earliest theological era, there was a certain element of positive science, that is, of knowledge of the permanent relations of things. The most arbitrary will is not all arbitrary, but presupposes something of a fixed order without or within, and therefore the anthropomorphic analogies by which phenomena were interpreted, still left some space for the idea of law. And this space was continually being widened, at the

expense of the arbitrary and the accidental.
While metaphysics seemed simply to be substituting one transcendent explanation for another,
it was really disguising the abandonment of all
transcendent explanations whatever, and the
introduction of positive explanations in their
place. The doubts expressed in the metaphysical
criticism were really due to a growing sense of
law, which, when it became clear and self-conscious, produced the positive philosophy. Hence
there was, for a long time, an intimate alliance
between the scientific and the metaphysical spirit,
though the former was merely "*critical*," and the
latter "*organic*." And this alliance was the more
easily maintained, because, in the first instance,
neither the negative character of the former nor
the positive character of the latter was distinctly
discerned. Metaphysic was not seen to be merely
"critical," because its abstractions were taken to
be real entities. And science could not be seen
to be "organic," that is, to contain the principle
of a new organization of society, till it rose from
the contemplation of the inorganic world to the
study of life, and especially of human life. History, however, shows that science has always

reaped the fruits of every victory won over theology by metaphysic, and. on the other hand that metaphysic has never succeeded in maintaining any position against theology, which has not soon been occupied by science. The great metaphysical movement of the Greeks left for its sole permanent result the sciences of Geometry and Astronomy; while their premature speculations on Psychology and Sociology were suppressed or forgotten by the mediæval church, which directed all the intelligence of the world to the practical work of civilizing and organizing men by means of the monotheistic idea. When thought was again awakened, the abstract metaphysic of the Schoolmen was only the forerunner of the renewed study of natural science, especially of Physics and Chemistry, which at first appeared under the forms of Astrology and Alchemy; and the victory of Nominalism over Realism, in which the scholastic philosophy ended, was the indication of another triumph of the scientific spirit. For Nominalism is simply the negation of that tendency to personify abstractions, which is the essence of metaphysic. Finally, as a consequence of that development of science which culminated in Newton, metaphysic ceased to apply its method to the external world, and confined itself to the sphere of Biology and Sociology, from which it is now being gradually driven. In the last of these applications, its power for criticism and destruction, and its weakness for reconstruction and reorganization, were proved by the decisive experiment of the French Revolution, in which the ideas of the rights of man and the law of nature were tried and found wanting. Since that time political life has fluctuated between the theological and the metaphysical principles, and therefore between the opposite dangers of reaction and revolution, finding no security for order but in the former, and no security for progress but in the latter. But the advance of Sociology into the positive stage, which has been inaugurated by Comte, has, in his view, shown that the opposite interests of order and progress may be equally secured, if only we base both upon a knowledge of the laws by which the existence and activity of man are ruled, and not on the fictions of the imagination, or on the still emptier fictions of the understanding.

On science
the social
system of
the future
must be
based

The aim of the future, then, is one with the aim of the past. That social passion which in all great constructive periods of human history, and especially in the Middle Ages, took hold of theological beliefs and made them a means to organize and discipline mankind, is still to be the guiding motive of all speculation and action. But the system of thought which it uses for this end must inevitably be changed. Renouncing the theological and metaphysical interpretations of things, which have been proved to be either inconsistent with facts or at least incapable of being verified by facts, we must now base our effort to improve man's estate upon the laws of the resemblance, the coexistence, and the succession of phenomena as these are determined by science. And on the other hand, as we recognize that all the sciences tend to lose themselves in the multiplicity of a universe, where every path leads to the infinite, we must seek also to organize and discipline the hitherto dispersive efforts of science, so that they may be directed entirely to the relief and furtherance of man's estate. In this way scientific knowledge and social benevolence will act and react, at once limiting and supporting each other, and amid all the darkness of a universe which absolutely is unknowable, and, even relatively to himself, is only partially knowable, man can yet give a kind of unity and completeness to his transitory existence. For all he needs to know is that which experience has constantly been teaching, the uniformity and constancy of the laws of phenomena. By means of this know-ledge, so far as he can obtain it, and without any need to penetrate into the transcendent causes of things, he can foresee many phenomena, like those of the heavens, over which he has no control whatever, and also many phenomena, like those of his own nature and his immediate environ-ment, which he can, to a certain degree, change and modify. And thus he can learn, with con-tinually growing certainty, what are the means he must use to bring within his reach the highest good which the system of things allows him to attain, detaching his thoughts and interests more and more from the unfathomed abyss beyond, which he now knows to be by him unfathom-able.

Is it, then, possible for men to sketch out the programme of an existence limited to this "bank

Necessity for a new religion

and shoal of time," to conceive it as a complete
system in itself, and *ré-organiser sans Dieu ni roi,
par le culte systématique de l'humanité?*
they, surrendering the belief in "a Divinity that
shapes their ends, rough hew them how they will,"
"constitute a real providence for themselves, in
all departments, moral, intellectual, and material"?   Comte answers that they can; and
in the "Politique Positive" he tries to exhibit
the main outlines of that social system of the
future by which this end is to be attained.

His starting point is—strange as at first it
may seem—the idea of religion.   "Since religion
embraces all our existence, its history must be an
epitome of the whole history of our development."
Beneath and beyond all the details of our ideas
of things, there is a certain "esprit d'ensemble,"
a general conception of the world without and
the world within, in which these details gather
to a head.   If this conception or picture be co-
herent with itself, and if at the same time it be
such as to present an object on which our affections can rest, and an end in the pursuit of
which all our powers and capacities may be exer-
cised, then our life will have that unity and con-

*Religious
basis of
life.*

sistency with itself which is necessary for the highest efficiency and happiness. Such a harmony of existence, in which all its elements are fitly co-ordinated, is what, in Comte's view, constitutes a religion. And, since man is both an individual and a social being, this harmony is seen to involve two things. It involves a subordination of all the elements of man's individual nature to some ruling tendency, and it involves a certain adaptation of men to, and a combination of them with, each other. Further, this harmony of humanity with itself must also be a harmony of man with the world in which he exists. In other words, the individual can attain his highest perfection and happiness only in so far as he is, at once and by virtue of the same principle, in harmony with the world, with his fellow-men, and with himself.

Now, this harmony cannot be produced by the sway of personal or egoistic motives; for these are in fatal disagreement with each other, and they set each man in antagonism to all other men, and even to the natural conditions of his own existence. The regulation and harmonizing of the nature of the individual man, therefore,

Elements necessary for a religion.

implies his attachment or self-surrender to that which is without him, and to which he is necessarily related—to some object in that world of persons and things which hems him in on every side, and which must needs be his enemy so long as he is ruled by egoism. Further, if the principle of religion is thus to be found without and not within the individual man, it must be found in some object to which he submits as a superior power, and on which, at the same time, his affections can rest. Submission and love are both necessary to religion, for if we have merely the former, the utmost we can feel is resignation to a fatality; and this, though it involves a certain limitation of the selfish tendencies, can never overcome them, or substitute a new motive for them. To retain the energy of egoism and combine it with resignation to a power greater than ours, we must love that power to which we submit. Finally, this submission and self-surrender must be consistent with a certain relative sense of independence, for no feeling is really powerful which does not result in action. Hence, to submission and love, we must add the belief that we can make ourselves useful to that Being to whom we submit and whom we love. Only thus, when veneration for that which is above us, is combined with love for that which is the constant source of good to us, and with benevolence towards that which needs our help,* can we rise above the unreal and imperfect unity of selfishness into the perfect unity of religion. Or, to put it more shortly, in Comte's own language, "the principal religious difficulty is to secure that the external shall regulate the internal without affecting its spontaneity".; to secure, that is, that the free subjective principles of love and benevolence shall attach to the power to which we believe our existence to be subordinated. For if our faith be not one with our love, or if our love be not a principle of activity, we cannot be, in the full sense of the word, religious.

Now the difficulty of attaining such a harmony or unity of existence cannot but be obvious to those who live in a period when "the intelligence is in insurrection against the heart;" when what men desire and love is not by any means one with what, on the authority of science, they believe. If, however, we follow the course of

Scientific basis for religion.

---

* Cf. Goethe's "Three Reverences."

advancing knowledge, we shall see that this state
of things is merely temporary, and that completed
positive science gives us back all that in the
course of its development it seemed to take away.
Science, indeed, from its very dawn, when it discovers that there is a fixed order and law in the
movement of the heavenly bodies, gives support
to one element of religion, the sense that we are
in the hands of a superior power. It reveals to
man an ultimate necessity which bounds and determines his life—a necessity which, from the
nature of the case, he cannot modify. And as
the idea of law is gradually extended to physical,
chemical, and vital phenomena, this necessity is
seen to limit and control him on every side.
Phenomena, therefore, can no longer be regarded
as the expressions of the wills of fictitious beings
endowed with the qualities most admired in
humanity, and therefore capable of being loved.
And the natural effect of this is to reduce religion
into a mere resignation to an irresistible fate,
which is incapable of awaking or responding to
human affection. With the rise of sociology,
however, science changes its aspect, and begins to
restore to us more than all that was contained in

the dreams of mythology which it has destroyed. For this culminating science teaches us to regard the whole race of man as an organic and self-developing unity, in which we, as individuals, are parts or members. Between our own life and the merely external necessity of nature we see a spiritual power which modifies it and adapts it to our wants. Between the individual and the world stands humanity, and the " main pressure of external fatality does not fall upon the former directly, but only through the interposition of the latter." In passing through this medium, brute necessity is changed more and more into a saving providence. To be convinced of this we need only to observe that, after we go beyond the fixed order of the celestial system, which is the ultimate necessity of our lives, and which lies entirely beyond the reach of our interference, we come upon various orders of phenomena—physical, chemical, and vital—which are capable of modification, and are continuously subjected to it by man, and even by plants and animals. So soon as life begins, order becomes the basis of progress: for the living being not only adapts itself to the medium in which it lives, but continually reacts upon that medium, in order to render it more suitable for its wants; and in the case of man, inasmuch as his existence has a connection and a continuity that binds the whole race together through the long succession of ages, this reaction is cumulative. The life of the individual in any age is what it is, by reason of the whole progressive movement of humanity; and the later the time of his appearance the more he owes to his race. "The living are always more and more dominated by the dead." On this great benefactor, therefore, his thoughts can rest, as a power which moderates and controls his whole life, and which controls it not merely as a fate to which he must resign himself, but as a providence to which his love and gratitude are due. Nor will such feelings be less powerful because this Providence is one which he can serve, and which needs his service. Hence he is led to contemplate his life in all that makes it worth living, as the gift of a "Grand Être," to whom during his short term of earthly years it is his highest virtue to devote himself, and with whom it is his final reward to become incorporated. For his "*objective*" or actual existence

in time has no valuable result, unless it add
to the "*subjective*" existence of humanity, the
influences and memories which mould for good
the lot of subsequent generations. His religion,
in short, is to consider himself as a useful link
in the chain between the past and future of
the race, a soldier of humanity in the continual
struggle whereby it adapts itself to its sphere
of action, and its sphere of action to itself, so
as to realize an ever richer and more harmonious social existence.

It is true indeed that Humanity has no absolute power, that it is hemmed in by a fatality
which it can only partially modify. "This immense and eternal Being has not created the
materials which its wise activity employs, nor
the laws which determine the results of its
action." But it is as vain to attempt to raise
our hearts beyond this immediate benefactor, as
to carry the mind beyond the circle of experience
within which it is necessarily enclosed. Nay, it
is not only vain, but hurtful. "The provisional
régime which ends in our day has only too clearly
manifested the gravity of this danger, for during
it the greater part of the thanks addressed to the

Humanity
the only
true God.

fictitious Being constituted so many acts of ingratitude to Humanity, the sole author of the benefits for which thanks were given." " If the adoration of fictitious powers was morally indispensable, so long as the true 'Grand Être' that rules our lives could not clearly manifest himself, now at least it would tend to turn us away from the sole worship that can improve us. Those who would prolong it at the present day are forgetting its legitimate purpose, which was simply to direct provisionally the evolution of our best feelings, *under the regency of God during the long minority of Humanity.*" Of this worship, the Christian doctrine of the incarnation might be regarded as an anticipation, and still more perhaps the mediæval worship of the Virgin; for women, as the sex characterized by sympathy, are the fit representatives of Humanity. They mediate between Humanity and man, as Humanity mediates between man and the world.

The social system based on this religion.

But the worship of Humanity is only the general principle from which the new life of " Sociocracy " must spring, it is not " Sociocracy " itself. We have therefore to inquire what is the order of life that corresponds to this new religion.

How does it modify our ideas of the relation of men to each other and to the world? And what light does it cast upon the various forms of social existence, upon the Family, the State, and the Church? I can only give a brief *résumé* of Comte's answers to these questions.

All civilization or improvement depends ulti- mately on man's control over material resources, over the powers and products of nature. And, on the other hand, it is the reactive influence upon himself of the effort by which he appropriates and adapts these resources to his purposes, which first civilizes and educates him. Man can only conquer nature by obeying her laws, and to obey these laws he must know them. Hence it is the necessities of the practical life which excite the first efforts after scientific knowledge, and it is under the pressure of the same necessities that man first learns to surrender self-will to the discipline of regular labour, and of co-operation with his fellows. We might indeed imagine a different kind of education for the human race. If mankind generally, like some of the richer classes, were placed in circumstances in which, without effort or struggle, they could at once

C

Marginal note: Man in conflict with nature.

satisfy all their natural wants and desires, we
might imagine that social sympathies and intellectual tastes would soon prevail over all the
personal or egoistic tendencies. For though the
latter were at first far the strongest, they would
gradually die out for lack of occasions for exercise. Losing thus the powerful stimulus of self-
interest, which drives us to investigate the laws
of nature, the intellectual activity of such beings
would take an æsthetic direction, and would be
devoted mainly to the task of providing forms
of expression for the social sympathies. These
social sympathies would become intense, for they
would occupy the whole of life. But they would
in the first instance be confined in the circle of
the family ; for the social life of States gains
its principal interest from the ever-widening co-
operation which is required in the struggle for
existence against external difficulties. The natural creed of men would be an æsthetic Fetichism ; and this, in the course of time, when men
had learned to distinguish between action and
life, would be changed into Positivism without
needing to pass through the long intermediate
stages of theology and metaphysics ; while, in

the practical life, the affection of the family would broaden to the love of humanity, omitting the middle term of nationality. Finally, as the heart and the intelligence would continually gain a more marked ascendency over the practical activity, it would be natural that the spiritual power should rule the temporal, and that women should have the supremacy over men.

This ideal, however, only serves to illustrate by contrast the real course of things, which indeed continually advances towards the same goal, but by a far longer and more stormy path, a path not of untroubled and peaceful growth, but of conflict, division, and pain. We shall find, however, as a kind of recompense for this hard process of mediation, that the final reconciliation of humanity with the world and with itself is far more perfect and conclusive, as it is a reconciliation which subordinates, while it satisfies, all the different elements of his nature. For a "sociality," reared on the basis of a fully developed yet conquered "personality," is a far higher ideal than such an imagined paradise, in which the struggle for existence, with all the intellectual and physical

Uses of this conflict.

exertion which it involves, would be made unnecessary.

It awakens and disciplines his moral nature.

Our personal tendencies are strongest at first, and in their direct action they might lead, and do indeed often lead, to a sacrifice of society to the individual, and to the development in him of an extravagant pride and self-will, by which both heart and reason are corrupted. But man soon finds that he must stoop to conquer; that he must submit his action to the laws of nature, if he would make nature the servant of his purposes; that he must himself be instrumental to the well-being of others ere he can make them instruments of his own well-being. And in this submission of caprice and passion to reason and law, and of his own life to social ends, he gradually developes his intellectual powers and social sympathies till they gain a supremacy over those egoistic tendencies to which in the first instance they were subordinated. The highest ideal of man's life is to systematize this spontaneous process, and to turn into a conscious aim that moral and intellectual discipline of his nature, which in the past has been the unforeseen result of his effort after personal ends. We must, however, remember that this result would not have been possible unless the beginnings of these higher tendencies had existed in man from the first. No empirical process could ever have developed social sympathies in him, if he had been by nature utterly selfish, any more than it could have produced reason in a being who was devoid of even the germ of intelligence. But the whole history of human progress is just an account of the process whereby feeble social affections, using as a fulcrum the outward necessities of man's life, gradually secure to themselves the direction of all his activity. "The principal triumph of humanity consists in drawing its best means of perfecting itself from that very fatality which seems at first to condemn us to the most brutal egoism." For, "so soon as the personal instincts have placed us in a situation proper to satisfy our social tendencies, these, in virtue of their irresistible charm, commonly guide us to a course of conduct which they could not have had at first the force to dictate."

These principles find their illustration in cer- *Economical and social progress.* tain economical truths. In most conditions in which human beings are placed, the individual is capable of producing more than is immediately necessary for his wants ; or, in other words, of accumulating wealth. Such accumulations make social existence possible, and coming, by gift or conquest, into the hands of the heads of society, become the means of realizing a division of labour, and providing the different classes of labourers with sustenance and instruments of production. Division of labour, again, while it secures increased efficiency, makes continually greater demands upon science for guidance, and thus stimulates the development of the intellectual life. Thus the hard external conditions under which man has to seek the satisfaction of his wants become a beneficent necessity, which forces him to increase his knowledge, and to co-operate with an ever-widening circle of his fellow-men. This co-operation, indeed, is not always conscious ; and, even when it is conscious, it is not necessarily accompanied by social sympathy, as is shown by the fierce industrial struggles of capital with labour at the present day. Yet it is inevitable that it should in the long run produce a sense of the solidarity of mankind. " As each one really labours for the others, in the end he must acquire the consciousness that he does so labour," and the consciousness of being a part in a greater whole must produce a willingness to serve it and live for it. Thus, a movement beginning in the reactive influence on man's activity of the physical conditions of his life, extends its effects gradually to his intelligence and his heart, so that the order of the elements of his nature becomes, as it were, inverted ; the first becomes last, and the last first. And, instead of the self-concentration of the savage, we have the development of a social impulse, which begins by setting the family before the individual, which goes on to set the state before the family, and which must end in setting humanity before all.

The way in which this movement is accomplished, and the form of social life in which it must result, are determined by principles that have already been suggested. The abstract elements of human life, of which we are to take account, are material, intellectual, and moral force, corresponding respectively to the will, the intelligence, and the heart. And these again correspond to three forms of association among men—the

The three forms of society.

State, the Church, and the Family ; three partial societies, in the union of which alone man can attain the complete satisfaction of his complex being. It is scarcely necessary to intimate, however, that this general correspondence of the abstract and concrete divisions is not meant to imply that any one of these forms of society is purely material, purely intellectual, or purely based upon affection. The great whole of the universal society is made up of parts which are like it, and are themselves wholes ; and in every one of them we can make a division of material, intellectual, and moral powers. Still, with this reservation, we may say generally that the bond which holds the family together is one of affection ; that the bond of the state is one of action, or material purpose ; and that the bond of humanity is the spiritual bond of intelligence. And further, that, as in the Family the tone and temper of the whole society is determined by the women, so the tone and temper of the State is determined by the practical classes, warlike or industrial ; and the tone and temper of the Church by the priesthood, theological or scientific. It is one main design of Comte's sociology to organize and put

in their proper relation to each other the three
great social powers, which have successively established their claims in the long history of
human development. The dawn of civilization
saw the organization of the family, under the
guidance of Fetichism. Polytheism taught men
to combine in a civil society, under the guidance
of a power in which temporal and spiritual authority were confused together. Finally, Monotheism separated the secular and spiritual powers,
and established a certain provisional equilibrium
between them. Metaphysic was powerful only
to destroy; but by sapping the foundations of
the theological system it prepared the way for
Positivism, by which Family, State, and Church
are finally to be distinguished and harmonized,
or fixed in their proper organic relations to each
other, so as to preclude for ever their warfare or
intrusion upon each other's provinces.

In determining the nature and relation of these
three forms of social union, Comte lays down two
principles. The first is, that there can be no
society without a government, any more than
there can be a government, or effective power
among men, without a society. "A true social

force is the result of a more or less extended co-operation, gathered up into an individual organ." It is a result in which many are concerned, yet which finds its final expression through the will of one. As to the former point, that a social basis of force is necessary, Comte says that " there is nothing individual, except physical force," and even physical force is very limited when it is merely individual. Every other kind of power, whether intellectual or moral, is essentially social, dependent on the co-operation of many minds in the present, and generally also on a slow accumulation of energy in the past. As Goethe said, " It is not the solitary man that can accomplish anything, but only he who unites with many at the right time." Nor, on the other hand, can we have social force without government. The concurrence of many can never be really effective, until it finds an individual organ to gather it up, and concentrate it to a definite result. Sometimes the individual comes first, fixes his mind on a determinate purpose, and then gathers to himself the various partial forces which are necessary to achieve it. More often in the case of great social movements,

there is a spontaneous convergence of many particular tendencies, till, finally, the individual
appears who gives them a common centre, and
binds them into one whole. But in all cases
the effective co-operation, the real social force, is
not present till it has thus concentrated and
individualized itself.

The second principle is one that has been
already illustrated. It is, in Comte's view, the
law of the world that the higher should immediately subordinate itself to the lower. Thus
the organic finds its life controlled and limited
by the inorganic world, and man has to work
out his destiny in submission to all the necessities, physical, chemical, and vital, which are presupposed in his existence. The higher, therefore,
can overcome the lower only by obedience; if it
is to conquer, it must at least "stoop to conquer."
And this law holds equally good in the case of
the social life of man. As it is the satisfaction
of material wants that is, and must be, the first
motive of his life, so it is in the effort to maintain his outward existence, and to employ the resources of nature for the satisfaction of his desires,
that his powers are first excited and disciplined.

Outward subordina-tion of higher to lower.

Hence it is the practical activities—military or industrial according to the state of civilization —which must bear the immediate rule in his life; not because they are the highest, but because they are the indispensable basis of everything else.   Moral and intellectual influences can only come in afterwards, in the second place, to modify the ruthless energy of the practical life. They are essentially restraining, correcting, guiding, and not in the first instance stimulating or originative forces.   It is when they act in this indirect way that they are really most efficient, and their direct action, if it were possible, would defeat itself.   Their purity cannot be secured except by their withdrawal from the sphere of action and command; their power is dependent on their self-abnegation and rejection of immediate authority and rank.   They cease to influence men when they begin to dominate. Nay, even if their purity were secured, and they could reign without rivals, we have seen that they would produce a less beneficent result than when they come in as moderators.   The purely " altruistic " and intellectual being, in whom personal motives did not exist, would have a less exalted ideal of life set before him than one in whom the personal motives exist in all their energy, but are remoulded in conformity with social interests.

On this basis we have to consider the order The Family. of the Family, the State, and the Church. The family is the first instrument of man's social education. It takes him at the lowest point, to raise him to the highest. Its life is the "only natural mediation which can habitually disengage us from pure personality, to raise us gradually to true sociability." In it the man, according to the above principle, must bear rule, though it be the woman, who, "*par l'affectueuse réaction du conseil sur le commandement,*" ultimately determines the spirit of the society. A shadow also of the other spiritual power, the power of intelligence, often appears in the family, especially in the early patriarchal societies, in the customary authority given to the moderating counsel of the elders who are beyond the age for active service.

The State is the peculiar sphere of the active The State. or secular power, which, after being military, has now become distinctly industrial. During the military stage, the harmony of the different classes in the State was less difficult to preserve, seeing that common danger bound together the soldier classes, and confirmed their fidelity to their - leaders; while, in general, the industrial offices were committed to slaves or serfs, who were deprived of all political power. The change to an industrial order of political life brings with it many dangers to the unity of the State, especially as it has taken place at a time when the old theological basis of belief is undermined. Hence the already difficult task of organizing society, on the basis of individual freedom and without the external pressure of danger, is rendered still more difficult. The capitalists, who are the natural leaders of an industrial society, have often been wanting in the consciousness of their social function, and in their conduct towards their workmen, and towards each other, have been given up to the action of personal motives. On the other hand, the labourers, or "proletaires," filled with the new sense of independence and excited by revolutionary doctrines of individual right, have lost the sense of loyalty, and have filled their minds with Utopias of equality, which really involve the negation of the division and co-operation of labour—*i.e.*, of all social organization. The aim of all social reform, therefore, must be to bring back that willing subordination to leaders inspired by the sense of social duty, which characterized the military régime in its best form. But this, in the decay of theology, and the consequent loss of influence by the Catholic Church, requires the development of a new social doctrine based upon science, and the rise of a new spiritual power to teach and apply it to modern society. The State cannot be perfectly organized without the revival of the Church, for it is the wider spiritual unity of humanity that alone can give renewed strength to the bonds of material order in the State.

The great achievement of the Middle Ages *The Church.* was the separation of the spiritual from the temporal power. This has often been taken as a historical accident, but really it was the necessary expression of the true relation of theory and practice, which, in their demands and requirements, are essentially opposed, and which therefore cannot be fully developed except in relative independence of each other. Theory is general, and cannot attain its highest point unless it is universal. Practice is particular, and its greatest success is the fruit of concentration upon special circumstances and objects. Theory therefore becomes stunted, and loses its freedom and impartiality, if it is brought into close connection with the narrower aims of the outward life. Practice, on the other hand, loses little by the egoism of personal will and desire, and, indeed, within proper limits requires it. To gain the full benefit of this distinction, we must adopt with all its consequences the mediæval division of clergy and laity, Church and State. On the one hand, therefore, we must reduce the State to the dimensions of a city, with its proper complement of rural domain, "for experience has proved that the city, when completed, and sufficiently supported by material resources, is the largest political society that can be produced and maintained without oppression"; as it is also the society which secures the most definite and specialized reaction of man's social activity on the physical medium by which he is surrounded. Further, within the city so constituted, we must have as intensive a division of labour as possible, the government being concentrated in the hands of those capitalists whose occupations are of the greatest generality (*i.e.*, the bankers); the other capitalists (merchants, manufacturers, and agriculturists) taking their rank according to the same principle; and the proletaires following, organized in fraternal equality. Finally, the various offices are to be handed down from one generation to another according to the principle of "heredité sociocratique," each official choosing his successor, subject to the approval of his superiors; for this, and not the anarchic principle of the choice of superiors by inferiors, is the true modern principle of government, which succeeds to the old method of inheritance by birth. On the other hand, the order of the priesthood is to be in everything the exact opposite of the order of the laity. In the first place, motives of personal interest are to be excluded, so far as possible, from their lives. There is to be no competition of trade among them, but all spiritual work is to be paid by salaries from the public, and these salaries are to be fixed at so low a rate, even in the case of the highest members of the order, that there shall be no inducement to enter the order from motives of cupidity.   In the second place, although there will necessarily be a certain subordination of rank, in order to secure discipline and combined action, and all the priesthood will be arranged in a hierarchy under the "grand Prêtre de l'Humanité," yet there must be no specialization of function, or division of labour among them.   The modern anarchy of science is, as Comte maintains, due to the fact, that scientific men are mostly specialists; and *his* priests therefore are to be trained in all science, from mathematics, through physics, chemistry, and biology, to sociology and morals—for which last all the other sciences are to be regarded as preparatory. In this way the "esprit d'ensemble" will prevail among them, and science will be preserved from its present uncertain aberrations into regions from which no gain can be brought back for the furtherance of humanity.   Nay, Comte appears to regard even the separation of Art from Science as a step toward anarchy, and demands that his priesthood should be the artistic as well as the philosophic teachers of men.   At the same time they must avoid, as the most fatal source of corruption, all tendency to interfere more directly in practical affairs. Their business is to "modify the wills, without ever commanding the acts of men," and they cannot preserve the universality which is their characteristic without a complete renunciation of the right to compel. The farthest point to which they may go in this direction, is to excommunicate, or affix a social stigma on offenders; which, however, in a positivist society, will be a sufficiently severe punishment.

Such a priesthood will be the natural representatives of the unity or solidarity of mankind, as opposed to the particular interests of individuals and classes. They will also be the representatives of the continuity of the life of humanity, in the past and the future, as opposed to the excessive claims of the present hour. It will be their duty to make men conscious that their occupations are social functions, and that everything that is valuable in their lives has been gained for them by the long-continued labours of humanity, whose gratuitous gifts it is their highest privilege to preserve, and hand down increased by their own contributions to posterity. The

The priesthood of humanity.

clergy will thus be, as in the old system, the natural allies of the women; for what they have to do is simply to generalize and support, by a complete scientific view of the world and of human life, those lessons of the heart which are first learned by man in the narrower circle of the family. By their encyclopædic view of knowledge, the intelligence, which under the dispersive régime of science has become a rebel against the heart, is to be brought back to its allegiance, and the civic and human relations to be reconstituted on the type of the family.

The practical work of the Church. In impressing such a view of life upon mankind, the Positivist Church will avail itself of all the aids of art, and will use the power of imagination to fill up those voids and imperfections which sober science . undoubtedly leaves in our knowledge of things. For it is the function of poetry not merely to give body and substance to the necessarily abstract ideas of science; it may even, justifiably, outrun the possibilities of knowledge, though in that case we must not forget the unverified nature of . the illusions to which we yield. In the first of these uses Art will give precision and force to the worship of Humanity, or of its representative—Woman. It will provide language for those exercises of prayer and praise, by which we make vivid and real to ourselves our union with others, and dedicate ourselves to a life of "Altruism." It will thus intensify and deepen the *subjective* life, through which past humanity lives in us, and enable us to look forward with joy to our only personal reward, that of being incorporated in Humanity, and living again in the subjective life of others. For "*toute l'éducation humaine doit préparer chacun à vivre pour autrui, afin de vivre dans autrui;*" which is the true social doctrine of immortality, as opposed to the anti-social doctrine of an *objective* immortality for ourselves. The other use of poetry, in which it transcends the strict limits of science, is to revive something like the early fetichist belief that everything lives and is moved by human desires and affections. Thus, as a matter of fact, the inorganic world, so far as we know it, is governed by a fatality which is indifferent to the well-being of man. Nay, in its first action, it seems to call forth those tendencies in us which most need to be repressed and subdued. And it is only by the providence of Humanity that this very hostility and opposition of Nature are made instrumental to the attainment of a higher good. Yct, the victory being won, we may be allowed, at least in poetic rapture, to forget the discord between man and the world he inhabits; or to regard it as existing only with a view to that higher good which has resulted from it. For, "*l'existence humaine ne s'informe guère du temps qui exigea sa préparation spontanée.*" When we consider Nature as summed up in man, we learn "to love the natural order as the basis of the artificial order," produced by humanity, "so as to renew, under a better form, the fetichist affections." In his last work, Comte carries this extension of poetic license to its farthest point, and bids us add to our adoration of humanity, as the "Grand Être," an adoration of space, as the "Grand Milieu," and of the earth, as the "Grand Fetiche"; and he would have us think of these two as yearning for the birth and development of Humanity. In Comte's system, therefore, as in a more familiar text, "the earnest expectation of the creature waiteth for the manifestation of the sons of God"; and that optimism, which is rejected at the beginning as truth, is brought in at the end as poetry. Only, poetry is not, as with the Apostle, the anticipation or foretaste of knowledge; it is the substitute provided because knowledge is absent and unattainable.

For our purpose it is not necessary to go beyond this point. The minute prescriptions of the fourth volume of the "Politique Positive" add little or nothing to the general meaning of the system. The positivist New Jerusalem is as definitely determined and measured as the Holy City of the Apocalypse; but the main interest of such details is for the church and not for the world.

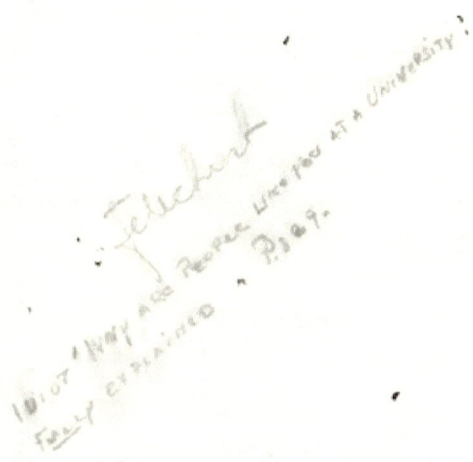

CHAPTER II.

THE NEGATIVE SIDE OF COMTE'S PHILOSOPHY—HIS OPPOSITION TO METAPHYSIC AND THEOLOGY.

*Growth of a new view of the social organism opposed at once to
Individualism and Socialism—Comte and the German Idealists
—Meaning of his attack on Metaphysic—His real agreement
with modern metaphysicians—He adopts Locke's principles
as to knowledge, yet is opposed to the Individualism of Locke's
French disciples—He attacks Religion as a Nominalist and
Nominalism as a Realist, and is really guided by a higher
principle than either—His mistaken attitude towards the
Critical Philosophy—Relation of Philosophy to Science—It
makes men conscious of their guiding principles—Comte's unconsciousness of the categories that guide his thought—Consequent defects in his view of the development of Religion, of
Philosophy, and of Science—Mr. Spencer's criticism and
Littré's answer—Ambiguity in the opposition between the
universal and the particular.*

IN the previous chapter I have given a sketch
of Comte's system, and especially of that part of
it which has attracted least attention in this
country—the social philosophy of the " Politique

Positive." In this and the subsequent chapters I propose to make a few criticisms on the system, with the view of exhibiting the fundamental tendencies of thought which are manifested in it, and of contrasting the manifestation of those tendencies in Comte, with their manifestation in other writers, especially in the great German idealists of the beginning of this century, In these criticisms I shall observe the same relative limitation as in the previous chapter, and shall give most attention to the social and religious results of Comte's philosophy. As, however, it is impossible to separate these from the philosophical principles upon which they are based, it will be necessary, in the first place, to examine the ideas of Comte as to the development of human thought in general, and of science in particular.

Comte, like every great writer, was a son of his time; and his greatness is measured by the degree in which he brought to articulate expression the ideas which were unconsciously, or half consciously, working upon the minds of those around him. The great emancipating movement of thought in the eighteenth century, which found

Tendency of Comte's time to a new view of the social organism.

its clearest expression in the works of Hume and
Voltaire, and which was kindled into revolutionary passion by Rousseau, awakened, by way of
reaction, an equally extreme movement both in
theory and practice, toward the reassertion of
authority and social order.   But in the midst of
this flux and reflux of the popular consciousness,
and still more after the extreme limits of each of
these movements became clearly marked, a new
idea was gradually taking possession of all minds
that could rise above the atmosphere of party.
Emancipation, pushed to the extent of isolating
the individual from that general life through
which alone he can become a moral, or even a
rational being, and rebellion, pushed to the extent of severing the present from that past upon
which it is necessarily based, had for their natural
counterparts an equally exaggerated panic of reaction, and an equally indiscriminate admiration
of past forms of thought and life.   Even in Rousseau the idea of savage isolation is crossed by
longing reminiscences of the patriarchal state, and
of the republics of antiquity; and the romantic
spirit, with its revival of mediæval types and
models, soon began to spread through the litera-

ture of Europe, and to affect its social and political
life. Between these opposing tendencies the conception of society as a unity, yet not a mechanical +
but an organic unity, of living and independent
members, presented itself as the reconciliation of
socialism and individualism, or, in other words,
of the opposing interests of unity and freedom.
And with this came another kindred idea—
the idea of development or organic evolution—
which made it possible to admit men's obligations to the past without denying the claims of
the present and the future. Condorcet, Kant,
and Edmund Burke are three writers of very
different temper and tendency, but in all of them
we find this consciousness of the organic unity
and evolution of the life of men and nations.
All equally oppose the crude theory of a Social
Contract and recognize that the unity of the
State or of Society is something better "than a
partnership agreement in a trade of pepper and
coffee, calico or tobacco, or some other such low
concern, to be taken up for a little temporary
interest, and to be dissolved by the fancy of the
parties;" that it is, on the contrary, "a partnership in all science, a partnership in all art, a

partnership in every virtue, and in all perfection." All equally recognize that the social state, to which they look forward as the ideal of the future, cannot be merely an historical accident, or a success achieved by the skilful contrivance of individuals; but that it must be the final realization of a principle, which has been working through all the past history of man, and which has underlain not only the old order of European civilization but also the movement of rebellion against it.[*] Finally, after Kant's suggestive, though imperfect, application of it to history, the same idea, with a deeper metaphysical perception of its meaning, became the central thought in the philosophies of Schelling and Hegel as early as the first years of this century.

Analogous tendencies in Comte and in the German Idealists

Comte, ignorant for the most part of the work of any except his French predecessors, was led to the same fundamental conception by the political experiences of France, as well as by the conflict of the opposite schools of Rousseau and St. Simon

---

[*] This is not strictly accurate, for Condorcet seems to except from his list of the elements of progress the whole social and ecclesiastical system which existed previous to the Revolution, while Burke can see no element of growth or improvement in the Revolution itself.

with each other and with the Catholic De Maistre. Yet, despite this independence, there is a certain parallelism between Comte's interpretation of the idea of development and that of the German idealists. That the first "Synthesis," or system of doctrine upon which man's intellectual and moral life is based, was poetic or imaginative; that it was therefore disintegrated and destroyed by the critical understanding; and that it requires to be restored and reconstituted on a rational basis, a basis which shall satisfy the a-wakened intelligence, as well as the heart and the moral sympathies—all this was a commonplace of German philosophy long before the advent of positivism.* The condemnation which Comte pronounced upon the individualistic and revolutionary theories of Rousseau is little more than an echo of the German attack upon the "Aufklär-ung." Even Comte's denunciation of the "meta-physical" explanation of the world by transcendent causes or "entities," which are not capable of empirical verification, and his assertion that man's knowledge is confined to the relative and

---

* Cf. especially Fichte's *Characteristics of the Present Age.* Many of Carlyle's characteristic expressions and ideas seem to have been suggested by this book.

phenomenal, finds a close parallel in the language of Kant. And Kant's idealistic followers, though they assert the possibility of a knowledge that goes beyond the phenomenal, do not assert it in the sense in which Comte denies it; for with them the negation of an absolute dualism between the noumenal and phenomenal is, as will afterwards be shown, only the necessary result of the doctrine of the relativity of knowledge itself. In all ways, therefore, the question between Comte and those whom he would have called metaphysicians is of a much more definite and specific kind than he or his followers have generally recognized. The general basis of thought—which belongs rather to the time than to any individual—is common to him with all the greater philosophic writers of his own, and even of the preceding generation. And the only point for controversy is whether he gave the most consistent and satisfactory development to those principles, which we cannot indeed say that he derived from others, but which he was certainly not the first to express. The question in short is, in the first place, how far Comte had a clear consciousness of the source and bearing of his own leading ideas; and, in the second place, how far he has been successful in applying them. I venture to think that in both points of view a careful examination of his works shows him to be defective. He fails to apprehend with clearness the logic by which his own thoughts are guided, he fails to follow out that logic to its legitimate result, and his system, therefore, with all its comprehensiveness, ends in inconsistency and self-contradiction.

In the first place, then, Comte's starting-point was fixed for him by the sensationalist philosophy of the last century. He begins where **Hume** ends, with the denial of the scientific value of metaphysics and theology. This denial he only modifies so far as to maintain that, while neither theology nor metaphysics can be regarded as forms of real knowledge, both must be regarded as necessary stages in the process by which real knowledge is attained. They are, in short, transitory forms of thought, which now survive only as stages in the culture of childhood and youth, or as prejudices in the minds of those who have not yet been awakened to the spirit of their time. Notwithstanding this wholesale rejection

Meaning of his attack on metaphysic and theology.

of metaphysic and theology, however, it may easily be shown that Comte's own theory, like every intelligible view of the world, involves a metaphysic, and ends in a theology; and that he only succeeds in concealing this from himself, because he is unconscious of the presuppositions he makes, because he uses the word "metaphysic" in a narrow and mistaken sense, and because he conceives it, as well as theology, to be bound up with a kind of "transcendentalism," which all the great metaphysicians of modern times agree in rejecting.

His real agreement with the modern metaphysicians.

Hostility to metaphysic, if by metaphysic be meant the explanation of the facts of experience by entities or causes, which cannot be verified in experience or shown to stand in any definite relation to it, is the common feature of all modern philosophy, idealist or sensationalist. It is as clearly manifested in Descartes as in Bacon, in Kant and Hegel as in Locke and Hume. If Bacon accuses the scholastics of anticipating nature by unverified hypotheses or presuppositions not derived from the study of nature, Descartes is no less emphatic in his denunciation of a philosophy of authority, and

in his demand for a fundamental reconstruction
of belief.   If the former bases all truth upon
experience, does not the latter seek the evidence
of his principles in the most intimate of experiences, the consciousness of self ?   Leibnitz is as
ready as Locke, Kant is as ready as Hume, to
maintain that philosophy must not introduce
transcendent principles into its explanations of
experience.   As Luther rejected a God who did
not reveal himself directly to the heart and intelligence of his worshipper, but only through
the mediation of a priest and in an external
tradition, so the greatest modern philosophers of
all schools are agreed in rejecting all principles
which do not find their evidence in being an
integral part of the experience of men.   It
would be too much to say that they all consistently develop this principle to its necessary
consequence, or that. traces of scholastic modes
of thought are not to be found even in those of
them who most strongly denounce scholasticism ;
on the contrary, it may be admitted that no
one before Kant saw what was involved in the
renunciation of the transcendent as an object of
knowledge.   Even Kant himself did not see all

E

its consequences. Still, the assertion of the principle itself, and the effort to realize it, is perhaps the most general and invariable characteristic of modern philosophy. In so far, therefore, as what Comte means by metaphysics is anything like the scholastic philosophy, with its transcendent or authoritative principles, no objection need be taken to his assertion that metaphysic is an exploded mode of thought, from which the philosopher and the man of science must now seek to free themselves. But then it must be added that, in this sense, none of the greater speculative writers of modern times is, in principle, a metaphysician ; and that the metaphysic which they cultivate is of a totally different nature. If, indeed, we could consider Comte's remarks as aimed at the great metaphysicians of his own day, at Kant and his successors, the description, and therefore the censure founded upon it, would be almost ludicrously inapplicable.

His antecedents.
Locke's
theory of
knowledge.

To understand the bearing of Comte's denial of metaphysics, however, we must keep in view his historical antecedents. This negation was, as I have already said, part of his heritage from the sensationalist philosophy of the last century, which had reached its most consequent and definite expression in Hume. It was a conclusion, the first step towards which was taken by Locke in his attack upon the Cartesian doctrine of innate ideas. In Locke's view, innate ideas were principles apprehended independently of all experience—possessions of the individual mind which it finds in itself at once, and apart from any process of development, or intercourse with anything but itself. And, to disprove their existence, it was enough for him to point to the fact that, prior to such intercourse with the world, the mind has no contents at all, and can scarcely be said even to exist. This obvious truth, however, was immediately confused by him with the doctrine that reality—the objective world of individual things as such—is immediately given in sense apart from any "work of the mind," and that any ideas or universals added by thought to the data of sense, must, *ipso facto*, be fictions. In making this assumption, Locke was yielding to a tendency of thought which had already shown itself in the nominalism of Hobbes. Locke, indeed, was not a nominalist, he was what is called a conceptualist; but in the Essay on the Human Understanding no distinct ground is ever stated for giving to universals more than that subjective value which even Hobbes allows to them. In his criticism of the ideas of substance and cause, Locke is always seeking to reduce fact and reality to the isolated sensations through which, as he supposes, individual things are given. And the same tendency of thought leads him also to regard the individual mind as apprehensive only of its own ideas and sensations, and excluded from all direct contact with the world. It soon, however, became obvious to the followers of Locke, that, on these terms, no knowledge, or even semblance of knowledge, is possible; that the individual mind, if it were thus confined to its own isolated feelings, could never dream of the existence of an objective world; and that to make possible the reference of sensations to objects, it is necessary that they should be connected together according to general principles. In other words, it became obvious that the universal, or some substitute for the universal, is required to make knowledge and experience possible. And to meet this want the theory of association was devised, and the atomic elements of the intelligible given in sense, were supposed to be linked together by the principles of resemblance, contiguity, and succession. It was not perceived that in these principles there is already implied the unity of the self-conscious intelligence, and, indeed, the whole body of categories which the theory of association is used to explain or explain away. It was the work of Kant to show this; to show, in other words, that the attempt to empty knowledge of its universal element must be suicidal, that it must be fatal not only to theology and metaphysics, but to all knowledge, even of the simplest facts of experience. But Hume—and it may be added most of his English followers, such as Mill and Mr. Spencer —halt half-way in the development of their sensationalism, and therefore think it possible to maintain, that while the ultimate reality of things is hid from us, because we cannot transcend our own ideas, we can still have knowledge of phenomena, because these ideas are combined in the minds of all men according to the same principles of association. It is from this point of view that Hume tells us that the principle of causality, based as it is upon mere association, may be fairly used to connect phenomena with each other, but that it is altogether insufficient to enable us to rise from phenomena to noumena —from the world to God. Thus the principles of the association of ideas are to the mind of man something like what wings are to the ostrich; they help him to run on the ground, but they are not strong enough to make him fly. As a succedaneum for that universal element in thought, which would raise us to the knowledge of things as they really are, they enable us to arrange the appearances—the shadows of our cave—and *that*, for the practical purposes of the cave, is all that we require.

And the social Atomism based upon it by the Encyclopædists.

While the English followers of Locke thus confined themselves to the development of his ideas on the theory of knowledge, his French followers seized upon his individualistic theory of existence, and used it as an instrument to undermine the Catholic faith, and the whole political and social system connected therewith. Diderot and D'Holbach found in Atomism the readiest weapon to assail the popular theology.

The former writer, indeed, sometimes plays with the atomic theory in a way that reminds us of the earth-shaking laughter of Aristophanes. In infinite time, he asks, in the infinite number of throws of the atomic dice, why should not, at one moment or another, a Cosmos spring out of chaos? and the Abbé Galiani can only hint, by way of answer, that, somehow or other, "les dés de la Nature sont pipés." Rousseau, applying the same idea to Sociology, proclaims the emancipation of the natural man, and develops the theory of the Social Contract, the theory which reduces the state to a creation of the individual will. Yet Rousseau had some uncertain glimpses of the truth that the individual has no rights or claims, except so far as he is an organ of the universal, and with strange inconsistency he declares, that it is only through social life that the human being "ceases to be a dull and limited animal, and becomes an intelligent being and a man."

Now it is curious that Comte, while in his theory of knowledge he accepts many of the ideas of the school of Locke, in his social theory takes up a position of intense hostility to the results of

He accepts the former, but not the latter.

the same philosophy.   That very individualism, which in Locke and Hume had been the ground and presupposition of the whole attack upon metaphysic, is assailed by Comte as the very essence of metaphysic.   "The metaphysical spirit," he is never weary of saying, "is radically incompatible with the social point of view;" it has "never been able to escape from the sphere of the individual."   From the empirical philosophy Comte accepted most of its negatives, especially its rejection of the possibility of metaphysics or theology as sciences of things in themselves, and its denial that even the principles, on which experience is based, are themselves derived from anything but experience.   But the school of Locke had generally denied the abstract universal in favour of the equally abstract individual, and here Comte declines to follow them. Individualism is seen by him to be an inadequate basis for social or even for biological theory, and the blame, as a matter of course, is cast upon metaphysics.   The "fate of metaphysical theory," he declares, "is decided by its inability to conceive of man otherwise than individually"; whereas "the true human point of

view is not individual but social." "Man is a
mere abstraction, and there is nothing real but
humanity, regarded intellectually and yet more
morally." * It is in fact just this thought of
the unity and the solidarity of man—not the
mere abstract unity of a genus, but the concrete
unity of one life, manifesting itself in many members—which enables Comte to look at the history
of the past in a way so different from most of his
predecessors, and to recognize the affinity of that
social synthesis of the future, which he himself
is trying to realize, with the previous theological
synthesis of Catholicism. It is this also which
leads him to create a new religion of humanity,
and even, in the end, to justify that poetic license
which seems necessary to complete the synthetic
view of life, and to bring nature into unity with
man. In the "Politique Positive" Comte's opposition to metaphysics as tending, in the language
of Burke, to dissolve society "into the dust and
powder of individuality," becomes even more
emphatic ; and with it is combined a continual
denunciation of the "dispersive régime" of the
particular sciences, which in the present day he

* Phil. Pos. vi. p. 692, Miss Martineau's Trans. ii. p. 508.

declares to be pursued by mere specialists, with an extreme waste of human faculty, and without any regard to the legitimate end of all science, the furtherance of man's estate. The conception of life and science, as a connected whole, all whose parts are to be estimated and developed in relation to each other, and to the idea of the whole, is by Comte as firmly held and as resolutely carried out to its consequences as by the most extreme idealist or pantheist. The only difference—which still shows the trace of the individualistic philosophy out of which Positivism was developed—is that the synthesis of Comte is, in his own language, *subjective*, not *objective;* by which he means that the whole, in relation to which all things are to be interpreted, and of which the individual man is to be regarded only as a part or member, is humanity, and not the universe. In other words, Comte holds that we transcend the limits of knowledge when we seek to regard ourselves as parts of the universal whole or system of things, and therefore as living under the providence of God; but that we do not transcend the limits of knowledge when we regard ourselves as parts of the one great organism of humanity, and therefore as living under *its* continual providence. We are not, as Berkeley and Hume had taught, confined to the phenomena of our individual consciousness; but neither are we capable of reaching a purely objective point of view. We can see things from the point of view of *a* whole, but not of *the* whole: at least we cannot so regard them except in that poetry of religion by which the earliest fetichist affections are renewed, and space and the earth are worshipped as the friends of Humanity. This, however, is mere poetic license; for we have no reason to believe that man has any friend but himself, and in its first direct action upon him the world shows itself to be anything but a system arranged for his benefit.

Now, without for the present discussing the truth of this view, we may remark that it is obviously the result of a compromise between the two opposite tendencies of thought, which divided the earlier history of modern philosophy. In the Cartesian philosophy there was a tendency— which manifested itself fully in the two greatest followers of Descartes, in Malebranche and Spinoza—to regard all things from the point of

He combines nominalism with realism.

view of the absolute unity of the Universe, and to treat the separate existence of the parts as a fiction of abstraction. On this view the individual's consciousness of himself as an individual is an illusion, and Spinoza would have said the same thing of his consciousness of himself as a member of the race. The only true consciousness is that in which both man and humanity are seen as absorbed in Nature, or, what is the same thing, in God. The followers of Locke, again, went so far in the opposite direction that they regarded the universal as a fiction of abstraction, and the individual as the sole reality. Hence they sought to confine the individual in *theory* to the perception of his own sensitive states, and in *practice* to the seeking of pleasant, and the avoidance of painful, feelings. Comte steers a path midway between the two extremes. To him, as to Locke and Hume, Nature is the vainest of abstractions, the last delusion of metaphysics; and all attempts to penetrate into the real being of things are the efforts of a finite creature to get beyond his own limits. Yet, on the other hand, to him, as to Spinoza, it seems irrational to separate the individual from the whole to which he belongs, and therefore, Humanity, instead of being regarded as a vague abstraction like Nature, is asserted to be the most real of all things or beings. "Man is a mere abstraction, and there is nothing real but Humanity." And Comte is so far from saying that the individual is confined to the data of his own individual consciousness that he rather maintains that we are unable to know ourselves, except as we know something else. Thus in criticizing the psychological method of internal observation—which, by the way, he supposes to be the essential method of metaphysics—Comte says:—" This pretended psychological method is essentially defective, for consider to what suicidal procedures it immediately leads; on the one side it bids you isolate yourself as far as possible from every external perception, and therefore prohibits you from carrying on any intellectual labour; for if you are employed in any, even the simplest calculation, what would become of the internal observation? On the other hand, after having finally by elaborate effort and arrangement attained this perfect state of intellectual slumber, you are called upon to watch the operations which are going on in your mind, when in fact there is nothing going on at all." * Comte sees the absurdity of a psychological method, in which the mind is isolated from the world and treated as one object among the others which have to be observed, instead of being regarded as a "part of all it knows," although he does not clearly indicate the source of the error. But the only result, as we have seen, is a compromise, in which the individual is supposed to be capable of objective knowledge, though only of phenomena, and capable also of objective aims, which, however, he cannot identify with the absolute end of all things. We can know, in Comte's opinion, not merely what is relative to our individual minds, but to the human mind ; and we can seek as our end, not merely our own individual pleasure but the happiness of Humanity. But we cannot know what things really are, apart from their appearance to us: we cannot worship any God who is in nature as in man, or identify ourselves with any divine purpose which reaches beyond the compass of this transitory existence, Whether

* Phil. Pos. i. p. 36.

this compromise is more than a compromise, whether it is a true solution of the difficulty, or a reconciliation of the opposite tendencies of thought in a higher unity, we have yet to consider.

The point, however, to which I wish here to call attention is, that Comte's protest against metaphysic loses almost all its weight because of his ignorance of the real scope and tendency of the metaphysical theories of the past, and of his own relation to them. He seems to have no perception of the essential distinction between the two tendencies of thought which he is partly opposing and partly reconciling. Beginning with a denunciation of metaphysic, because it treats universals as real entities, he ends by insisting on the truth that the Family, State, and Humanity, though *they* undoubtedly are universals, are at the same time objectively real. In the attempt to rise above the abstractions of earlier thought he is in harmony with the best metaphysics of his time. The defect lies in his unconsciousness of his own metaphysic, *i.e.*, of the categories which rule his thought, and which enable him to interpret the facts of experience,

He is really guided by higher principle than either.

and especially the facts of man's social life, so differently from his predecessors. For him, indeed, there is an easy explanation of this difference between himself and the philosophers of an earlier time. They were " metaphysical," while he is not ; they made assumptions, and substituted their own ideas for the teaching of experience, while he has simply made his mind into a mirror of nature, and stated the facts as they are. Comte forgets what his own principles led him on other occasions to perceive, that the world is what it is to us by the development of our own thoughts, and that we find in it only what we are prepared to find. Locke also, when he attacked the Cartesians, seemed to himself to be substituting experience for mere ideas, reality for fiction. He did not observe that he was substituting for the presupposition that the universal alone is real, the opposite presupposition that the individual alone is real ; and that the one presupposition is as much an idea as the other. And Comte, in his turn, guided by his new organic idea of social life and development, advances to the attack upon the individualistic philosophy, with the same naïve confidence that *his* idea is not an idea at all, but a fact. With all his talk of experience, he has never asked, or he has not understood the bearing of the Kantian question, What is experience? For if he had done so, he must have discovered that his own so-called positive thought was as metaphysical as that either of the Realists or of the Nominalists, and was indeed possible only as the result of a development which included both.

It is true that Comte in his " Politique Posi- His view of the critical tive " refers to Kant's criticism of experience, philosophy. though in a way that seems to show that his knowledge was derived only from hearsay. Kant is supposed by him to be a philosopher who first extended to the mind the general biological truth of the action and reaction of organism and medium upon each other. Because of this action and reaction, in which the mind modifies the object, as well as the object the mind, our thoughts do not correspond to the reality of things in themselves; they do not represent the medium as it is, but only as it appears to us, and our conception of the world is not therefore absolute, but only relative. On the other hand, we must not exaggerate this

F

truth so far as to suppose that the development of our thought is purely subjective ; or, in other words, that it belongs to the mind apart from the action of the world upon it (a view which Comte attributes to the German idealists). The true theory is "to regard the world as furnishing the matter, and the mind the form, in every positive notion. The fusion of these elements cannot take place except by reciprocal sacrifices. Excess of objectivity would hinder every general view, for generality implies abstraction. But the analysis which permits us to abstract would be impossible, unless we could suppress the natural excess of subjectivity. Every man, as he compares himself with others, spontaneously takes away from his observations that which is peculiar to himself, in order to realize that social agreement which constitutes the main end of contemplative life ; but the degree of subjectivity which is common to all our species usually remains, and remains without any serious inconvenience. Nor could we reduce its amount, except by intellectual intercourse with the other animals, an intercourse which is rare and imperfect. Besides, however we might restrict or diminish the subjective influences that mould our thoughts, in the effort to come to an understanding with intelligences unlike our own, still our conceptions could never attain to a pure objectivity. It is, therefore, as impossible as it is useless to determine exactly the respective contributions of the internal and the external in the production of knowledge." [*]

It is easy from this passage to see that Comte has not fully apprehended the bearing of the Kantian criticism. Kant does not seek to show that knowledge springs out of the action and reaction of subject and object on each other, but that there are certain universals, or forms of thought, by which the intelligence must determine the matter of sense ere we can know objects as such. The question which he discusses is, how experience, and objects of experience, as such, are possible. Kant would not, therefore, say that it is impossible " to determine *exactly* the respective contributions of the internal and the external in the production of knowledge ;" but that the problem is an absurd one, since subject and object are correlative elements

Kant's real view of knowledge.

* Pol. Pos. ii. 38

in the unity of knowledge, and not two separate
things, by the action and reaction of which upon
each other knowledge is produced. The unity of
experience is incapable of being transcended, and
it is a false abstraction by which we attempt to
take either subject or object out of that unity,
and seek to determine it as a thing in itself.
The *intelligi* and the *esse* of things are one, in
such a sense, that it is transcending the limits
of experience to attempt to determine either of
these apart from the other.* All knowledge or
experience implies and presupposes the unity of
the knowing mind and the categories through
which it determines its objects, and it is only in
virtue of these that there exists for us any
objective world of experience at all. Hence to
leave out the intelligence in our account of the
intelligible, to forget the constitutive power of
thought in speaking of existence (as is done by
materialistic and so-called empirical theories), is

---

*It is, no doubt, inconsistent with this that **Kant**
could admit the existence of a thing in itself, which
produces sensations in us, as in many passages he seems
to do. But it would carry us too far to discuss this
subject here. Comte, it may be admitted, could have
found many things in the letter of Kant to give plausibility to his view. Cf. below p. 124.

to mutilate and distort the essential facts of the case.

This Kantian view of nature and experience leads directly to certain important conclusions as to the work of philosophy. For, if its truth be admitted, it necessarily follows that the ordinary consciousness of men—even the ordinary scientific consciousness—is, in its view of the world essentially abstract and imperfect. The ordinary consciousness generally, we might even say invariably, deals with objects *as if* they were given independently of any thinking subject. It proceeds *as if* an intelligible world could exist without an intelligence, and thus leaves out of account an element, and indeed the most important element, in the facts of experience. And the business of the philosopher or metaphysician must be to correct the abstractness of ordinary, even of scientific, thought, to bring to clear consciousness the element which they neglect, and to determine how the new insight into the nature of knowledge, which by this process he has attained, must modify and transform our previous view of the objects known. In doing so, the metaphysician (or transcen-

Philosophy corrects the abstractness of science.

dentalist, as Kant calls him) is not introducing a new method; he is simply following the method according to which we are continually obliged to correct and complete the results of one science by another. Science is necessarily abstract, in so far as it investigates and determines certain aspects and relations of things, apart from their other aspects and relations. Thus, in geometry, abstraction is made of everything except the relations of lines and figures in space, in order that the spatial conditions of things may be fully determined, apart from their other conditions. And in like manner, "the dynamic laws of weight would still be unknown to us, unless we had first abstracted all consideration of the resistance, or the motion, of the atmosphere or other medium." The science of political economy is based on an effort to isolate, so far as is possible, the economical from all the other conditions of social life. In short, all the separate sciences, in this point of view, are abstract; and they tend to become more and more abstract as the scientific division of labour increases. That is, they tend to confine themselves to the investigation of certain definite **relations of** objects, leaving out of account all **their** other relations; or (what comes to much the same thing) to the examination of certain definite objects, without taking into account their manifold relations to other objects. Now, as Comte himself says, "these preliminary simplifications without which there could be no such thing as science **in the** true sense of the word, always involve a corresponding process of recomposition, **when** prevision of actual fact is called for." **To** attain a **complete** view of the **truth, we must return from the abstraction** of the isolated sciences **to** the unity of nature, in which all these separate objects and relations are brought together, and **in which they modify and** determine each other. **And** philosophy **only** goes a step farther **in the** same direction, when it corrects that abstraction from the thinking self, the unity of knowledge, which **is** common **to all** the sciences. The only difference is, that **the** abstraction **of** *science* from **the** unity **of the** objective world, as it is the result of a definite **act of** thought, **is generally** conscious; **while the** abstraction which *philosophy* seeks **to correct is** generally unconscious. The geometrician cannot

but see that there are other than spatial conditions of existence, and that, for his own purposes, he has left all such conditions out of
account.   But it is quite possible, as every
day's experience proves, to investigate the laws
of the intelligible world, without ever adverting
to its necessary relation to the intelligence, and
without being conscious of the abstractness of a
view of things, in which this relation is left out
of account.   Philosophy, therefore, has to detect
and bring to the light of day certain facts or
relations which enter into the constitution of
things, which indeed are presupposed in all
our consciousness of them, but which, nevertheless, generally escape without notice.   Of
this work of philosophy or metaphysics, however, Comte has no idea, or he confuses it with
the methods of an empirical psychology, which,
by an opposite abstraction, would separate the
thinking mind from the world to which it is
related.   But the method of philosophy is not
mere abstraction ; it is rather, if the expression
may be allowed, *concretion.*   Philosophy, as
Hegel said, is "thinking things together"—
i.e., thinking them in a unity that transcends

and explains their differences; or, if it ever abstractly considers the unity and movement of thought in itself, it is only (as geometry abstractly considers the relations of space) in order more surely and clearly to discern that unity and movement in all the objects of thought.

It is to Kant, principally, that this new way of stating the problem of philosophy is due; but it would be altogether a mistake to suppose that he essentially changed the problem itself. Metaphysicians, from the time of Socrates and Plato, have always sought to get beyond the presuppositions of the ordinary consciousness, and to remould that consciousness by bringing to light the principles upon which it rests. One of the best definitions that has been given of philosophy is "clear self-consciousness." And it is, indeed, just this character of metaphysical thought which renders plausible Comte's attack upon it. It is in the metaphysical writers of the past that we can most clearly discern the errors of the past, for by these writers the errors of the past are not merely implied and presupposed, but explicitly stated. Hence such writers are continually suffering from that natural illusion by which we

Metaphysic makes science conscious of its guiding principles.

take, as the prominent representatives of an idea
or tendency of thought, those authors by whom
it has been most distinctly expressed; whereas it
is rather they who first enable us, even if they
do not enable themselves, to see the limitations
of that idea or tendency, and to transcend it.
But as it is in the metaphysicians that we find
the clearest and most definite expressions of those
defective principles of past thought which we are
seeking to transcend, it is not unnatural that we
should attribute the defect itself to metaphysic.
What, however, is really due to metaphysic is
not the error, but rather that clearness and de-
finiteness of its expression which makes our refutation of it and our higher point of view possible. Thus the limit of Greek thought, the
point at which, by its own development, it falls
into error and self-contradiction, would have been
by no means so easy to discern, if its presuppositions had not been raised into ideal clearness
in the works of Plato and Aristotle. The individualism of the Stoics and Epicureans gives us a
key, which we would otherwise want, to those new
experiences of independence and isolation which
came to men under the Empire of Rome, after

the breaking up of the ancient municipal organization of social life. Descartes and Spinoza reveal the open secret of that new view of the relation of man to God, which was partly expressed by Luther and Calvin, and which was so powerful in moulding the political and social life, especially of Protestant countries, and in awaking in them a consciousness of individual and national independence, combined with a still more intense consciousness that the individual is nothing, except as the servant of a higher power. Hence it was in a criticism of these philosophies that Locke and Leibnitz found the starting-point for their fuller assertion of the claims of the individual. Finally, it is through a struggle with Individualism, especially in its fullest expression in Hume and Rousseau, that Kant and his successors in Germany, and Comte in France, were led to that higher organic idea in which the individual and universal cease to be opposed to each other as reality to fiction, and come to be regarded as different but complementary aspects of reality. If we no longer say, "The universal alone is real, and the individual is an abstraction;" or, "The individual alone is real, and the universal is a name;" but, "The individual is real, but only as the realization of the universal, and the universal is real, but only as manifesting itself in the individual," it is due to the whole past movement of philosophic thought. Nor, again, would it be difficult to show that the successes or failures of science at different times were closely connected with the sufficiency or insufficiency of the ultimate principles of thinking then acknowledged or presupposed. For it is the development of man's spirit which enables him to ask and to answer new questions in regard to the world of objects; nor can his growing knowledge of that world be separated from his growing consciousness of himself. To one who regards metaphysic from this point of view, its continual apparent failures will be as little suggestive of a despair of philosophy as the fall of the Greek State, or of the feudal system, is suggestive of a disbelief in the possibility of social and political life. It may even be said that no stage of culture, no limited form of human thought or existence, is ever completely exhausted and transcended, till it has risen to a clear consciousness of itself in a metaphysic, or

something of the nature of a metaphysic. It
is the disentanglement of the principle, the central idea, the fundamental category, which has previously ruled men almost without their knowing
it, that first enables them to see its value and
relation to that unity of the whole, with which
it was necessarily confounded so long as it remained merely a moving force in the depths of
the popular mind. Comte himself was metaphysical, in so far as he sought to transcend
the one-sided and imperfect categories of earlier
philosophy, and to reconcile them by means of
a higher thought. His defect lay in this, that
he was not metaphysical enough, that his analysis
of his own thought was imperfect, and that he
was therefore the instrument of a movement of
human intelligence, of the meaning of which
he was never clearly conscious. Otherwise he
would have perceived that his "positive" stage
was not simply a negation of the metaphysical
and theological stages which preceded it and a
return to fact and experience, but that it was
essentially a new reading of experience, which
implied, therefore, a new form of metaphysics
and theology.

Comte's
unconscious-
ness of his
own guiding
principles.

It is this unconsciousness of his own fundamental categories, which explains Comte's radical
misconception of the whole history of theology
and metaphysics.   The third stage of Positivism
is not the unity which transcends, while it reconciles, the previous stages of human development; on the contrary, it involves the total renunciation of those principles of thought which
had prevailed during the two previous stages.
According to this view, all that we can say is, that
a germ of positive thought existed from the first,
and that, by its development, theology and metaphysics were gradually driven from the whole
sphere of knowledge.   Positivism is thus the
concentration of human thought within certain
limits, which at first it did not respect, but which
it gradually learns to be, for it, impassable.   And
the only result of the process is, that the whole
field of the non-phenomenal is abandoned to
poetry, which is still to be permitted under
certain restrictions to fill up the vacant spaces
of the unknowable with shapes drawn according
to our wishes.   Theology and metaphysics are
but more or less thinly disguised anthropomorphisms, which once subserved a social pur-

pose, and which apart from that purpose have no
value for the intelligence; nor is there any element
of truth in them which needs to be preserved
under the new intellectual régime. Their history
was not a development, but a purely negative process—a process whereby they became attenuated
and dissolved, until the rich concrete meaning of
the first Fetichism had entirely disappeared in the
negations of the revolutionary philosophy. Monotheism, the last religion, was but the bare abstract residuum of theology, as the idea of Nature was the last abstract residuum of metaphysics. And the whole result of the long
striving of human intelligence to penetrate into
the absolute is merely the knowledge of its own
limits.

Now, it is not too much to say that this view
involves a fundamental misrepresentation, and
even inversion, of the whole history of religion
and philosophy. Its plausibility at first sight
arises from a common confusion as to the idea of
abstraction. In one sense it may be said that
there is no one so concrete in his view of things
as the child or the savage; in another sense, it
may be said that there is no one so abstract.

Consequent defect in his view of the development of religion

The mind of the child clings to the immediate images of things; it cannot rise above their pictured presence in space and time; it cannot sever them in thought from their immediate surroundings. On the other hand, the child's thought is abstract and simple; it confuses all things together; it scarcely distinguishes at first between animate and inanimate, between man and animal. With Comte we may call the child a Fetichist; not because his imagination raises all things to the level of man, but because he still lives in a simplicity or confusion of thought for which there are no distinct differences of level. On the other hand, as the child advances to maturity, the pictures of sense may partially fade, but his ideas of things become more complex and adequate. It ceases to be impossible for him to separate objects from the definite circumstances of space and time, in which they have been at first perceived; but at the same time, his knowledge of those objects, in their unity and difference—their permanent nature and their manifold phases and aspects—is continually growing. If, therefore, the movement of his thought, in one point of view, is toward greater

generality and abstractness, in another point of
view it is toward greater particularity and con-
creteness. To use a favourite modern phrase,
the development of human thought is by differentiation and integration, by induction and deduction at once. Now Comte's history of theology
and metaphysics is greatly distorted by the fact
that he detects in it only a movement of generalization and abstraction; and not also a movement towards greater complexity and completeness. Yet, even a superficial glance at the development of religion is enough to let us see
that the Christian idea of God in man is less
simple and abstract than Jewish Monotheism
or Oriental Pantheism. If indeed, we were to
judge of a religion by mere wealth of fantastic
sensuous symbolism, it might seem possible to
regard the earliest religions as the richest; though
even this might be disputed, seeing that the
fancy of the savage Fetichist, while capricious
and wayward, is at the same time singularly
monotonous and uninventive. But to any one
who would classify religions according to the
complexity and depth of the thought involved
in them, it must be apparent that they become

G

more full and definite——not more vague and simple——as time advances. Their progress toward greater universality is at the same time a progress toward greater specification. In the Indian faith we discern, from very early times, the presence of an idea of the divine unity. But it is a vague and abstract idea, and for that very reason it stands side by side with, or produces, a lawless Polytheism, in which there is neither method nor meaning; which, as Goethe says, does not subserve the true purposes of a religion, since it adds another chaotic element to life, instead of supplying a guiding principle through all its confusion and difficulty. In the Jewish religion we have a true Monotheism, in which the unity is no longer that of an abstract substance, but of a spiritual or self-conscious being ——a personal will which manifests itself in a definite purpose, in a moral government of men and nations. In Christianity, finally, we have the idea of a God, who is not merely an absolute substance——not merely a Creator and Ruler of the world, but a self-revealing Spirit; a Spirit who reveals himself in, as well as to, his creatures——an idea which combines in one the earlier

Pantheistic and Monotheistic conceptions. To regard the process in which these are three of the main stages as merely a process of abstraction and negation is surely to take a most external and superficial view of it. The truth is, that this and the similar sketch in Hume's " Dialogues on Natural Religion " are rather based on a preconceived theory as to the development of human thought in religion, than on the phenomena of religious history. And in Comte's " Social Dynamics," he has frequently to mention facts which are altogether inconsistent with it.

Nor is Comte's view of the history of metaphysic less fictitious and inaccurate. According to that view, the earliest philosophies ought to be the most concrete and complete, and the latest, the most simple and abstract ; but the very reverse is the fact. It is in the dawn of speculation that men are content to explain the universe by such abstractions as " being " and " becoming." The ancient philosophy contrasts with the modern, as simple with complex ; for while the former is occupied with questions about " the one " and " the many," the " universal " and the " particular," the latter is

Defect in his view of the development of philosophy.

concerned from the first with the relations of self-consciousness to the objective world. Again, confining ourselves to modern philosophy, we find the abstract Universalism (if we may use the expression) of Descartes and Spinoza, yielding in the next generation to two opposite forms of Individualism, and ending in the attempt of Kant and his successors "to read Locke with the eyes of Leibnitz, and Leibnitz with the eyes of Locke,"[*] and (we may add) to unite the elements of truth in both by a deeper view of the principle imperfectly expressed in Spinoza. In short, the whole movement of philosophy is a movement towards a more complex, and at the same time towards a more systematic, view of the world. Philosophical thought is ever seeking on the one hand to distinguish, and even to oppose to each other, the different sides of truth which were at first confused together; and again, on the other hand, to show that what were at first supposed to be contradictory, are really complementary, aspects of things. This progress of philosophy by differentiation and integration

* Green's Introduction to Hume.

Comte's theory does not explain, but it explains him. For, as has been indicated, Comte's whole view of the relation of the individual to society, and of the present to the past, manifests that same effort to concentrate and combine in one different and even opposed motives of thought which is shown in the idealistic philosophy of Germany. Only, as Comte is not conscious of this affiliation of his thought, but, on the contrary, supposes Positivism to be the simple negation of metaphysics, his possession of the higher idea shows itself, not in a new metaphysic, but only in a better comprehension of the social life and development of the race. Hence, also, he sees no positive connection between his own specula-tions and the previous history of philosophy, but connects it solely with the past progress of physical science.

This inadequacy of Comte's view of the his-tory of philosophy and theology leads to an opposite inadequacy in his view of the history of science. As the former is conceived by him to be a mere process of abstraction, which ends in nothing, so the latter is conceived by him— at least, in his first general account of it—purely

Defect in his view of the develop-ment of science.

as a movement from the abstract and general to the concrete and particular. There are thus two laws for the progress of the human mind—the law of its progress *to* science, and the law of its progress *in* science. The progress *to* science is merely the gradual destruction of the imaginative synthesis in which civilization began; the process *in* science consists in the gradual building up of the scientific synthesis in which civilization must end. Science begins with the consideration of the simplest and most abstract relations of things, with arithmetic and geometry, and it ends with the investigation of their most complex and concrete relations, with sociology and morals. This, with slight modifications, is the historical order of the genesis of the sciences, and, what is even more important in Comte's eyes, it is the order of their logical dependence or filiation, and therefore the order of a duly arranged scientific education. For each of the successive sciences—mathematics, astronomy, physics, chemistry, biology, sociology, and morals —includes a deductive part, in which it depends on previous sciences, and an inductive part, in which it makes a fresh start from experience

for itself; and **therefore no one can** be fully
equipped for **the** investigation of the more complex, who has not made himself master of the
laws **of** the simpler, phenomena. Like Plato,
Comte would write over the portals of science,
μὴ ἀγεωμέτρητος εἰσίτω, and he would add,——
Let no one enter upon the study of chemistry
who is not a master of the principles of physics ;
upon the study of biology, who is not a master
of the principles of chemistry; nor upon the
study of sociology, who is not a master of the
principles of all the previous sciences.

This view of the historical and logical filiation Mr. Spencer's criticism of that view.
of the sciences has been attacked with consider-
able force in an **Essay by Mr.** Spencer upon
the "**Genesis of Science.**" In that **Essay, Mr.**
Spencer points out, what, indeed, Comté himself
had very fully acknowledged, that *historically*
every science in turn has been an instrument
in the development of the others. Even in the
time of Aristotle politics and biology **had made**
no inconsiderable advance, while as yet physics
and chemistry could scarcely be said to be in
existence. And this is **only what** was to be
expected, for some knowledge of the conditions

of social order is a practical condition of the development of any other kind of science; and the necessary art of medicine forced men at a very early period to pay some attention to physiology. Astronomy had to wait for optics to furnish it not only with instruments but with definite conceptions of the dispersion and refraction of light; and physical investigation could not proceed very far without some kind of solution of biological and even psychological questions in relation to sense perception. It was the advance of geometry that led to the invention of algebra, and the transcendental analysis of Newton and Leibnitz was directly suggested by the problems of physics. These and many other facts of the same kind seem to show that a *serial* arrangement of the sciences misrepresents at once the historical order of their development and the logical order of their dependence. And in both points of view it would be nearer the truth to regard the different sciences (as Comte himself sometimes regards them) as " les diverses branches d'un tronc unique." For this " suggests the facts that the sciences had a common origin, that they have been developing simultaneously, and that they have been from time to time dividing and subdividing." Yet even this metaphor is inadequate, for "it does not suggest the yet more important fact that the divisions and subdivisions thus arising do not remain separate, but now and again reunite in direct and indirect ways. They inosculate; they severally send off and receive connecting growths; and the intercommunion has been ever becoming more frequent, more intricate, more widely ramified. There has all along been higher specialization that there might be a larger generalization; and a deeper analysis that there might be a better synthesis. Each larger generalization has lifted sundry specializations still higher; and each better synthesis has prepared the way for still deeper analysis."[*]

To these objections, Comte would probably have answered,[†] as Littré has answered for him, that there is a difference between the determination of some of the laws of a particular class of phenomena and the constitution of a science of these phenomena; and that a science cannot

Answer of Littré to Mr. Spencer.

---

[*] Spencer's "Essays," i. p. 145.

[†] Cf. Pol. Pos. i., *Introduction Fondamentale passim.*

be regarded as constituted till its inductive and
deductive parts are separated.   It cannot be
denied that physics involves all the relations
discussed in mathematics, and something more ;
that chemistry involves all the relations discussed in physics, and something more; that
biology involves all the relations discussed in
physics and chemistry, and something more ;
and that sociology involves the relations discussed in all the previous sciences, and something
more.   Now, it is a hopeless task for the weak
human intellect to deduce this " something more"
in the more complex, from the principles of the
less complex sciences, even if absolutely such a
deduction is possible.   Hence we cannot regard
a science as constituted, until its special subject-
matter has been separated from the subject-matter
of the simpler sciences, and until, in relation to
that subject-matter, certain laws have been determined which cannot be deduced from the
principles of those sciences.   Thus, in Comte's
opinion, biology was not constituted as a science
until, in quite modern times, the phenomena of
life were seen at once in their relative dependence on, and their relative separation from,

physical and chemical phenomena. **Nor** could
sociology be constituted as a science until, by
Comte himself, the law of social development
was determined, and the phenomena of human
life were thereby separated from phenomena of
life in general, which fall under the province of
biology. In this sense, therefore, it is argued
that the historical and the logical order of the
sciences are coincident ; and that, while it is
quite true that the advance of one of the
simpler sciences is often stimulated by requirements of the more complex sciences, it is equally
true that the more complex science has to wait
for the development of the simpler science, ere
it can rise above its first empirical stage.

It would be beyond the scope of this volume,
even if it were in the power of the writer, to
discuss in all their bearings these different views
as to the arrangement of the sciences ; but it
may be remarked that the most important of Mr.
Spencer's objections are directed, not against the
specific account which Comte gives of the historical and logical relations of the sciences, but
rather against his assertion that science progresses from the general to the particular, from

Ambiguity
of the opposi-
tion between
the universal
and the
particular.

the abstract to the concrete. That progress, he maintains, is "*at once* from the special to the general, and from the general to the special." If arithmetic comes before geometry, and geometry before physics ; on the other hand it is equally true, that geometry comes before algebra, and algebra before transcendental analysis, in which mathematics reaches its highest generalization. The " special " geometry of the ancients is contrasted by Comte himself with the " general " geometry of the moderns, and the Newtonian theory of gravitation was more general than the laws of Kepler, by the aid of which it was discovered. Now, looking at such illustrations as these by which Mr. Spencer supports his case, we cannot but think that the controversy really turns upon the ambiguity of " general " or " abstract," to which reference has been made ; and that in spite of what both Comte and his critic have said about the different meanings that may be given to these words, neither of them has consistently kept in view the difference between the " general " with which science begins, and that with which it ends. In one sense of the word, transcendental analysis is more "general" than arithmetic and algebra, but in another sense it is more specific. For transcendental analysis includes and explains both arithmetic and algebra, and casts its light even beyond their sphere; but it does so, not by becoming vaguer and less definite, but quite the contrary. It is a universal that does not leave out of account the differences of the particulars included under it, but rather determines them more fully. And the same thing may be said of the laws of Newton as contrasted with the laws of Kepler. It is easy enough to reach the general, if all that is wanted is a common element; for in that case we need only to abstract from everything but the simple idea of "being," and we have at one step reached the top of the logical tree of Porphyry, the highest universal of thought. But the universal of science and philosophy is something different from this; it is not merely a generic name, *under* which things are brought together, but a principle which unites them and determines their relation to each other. It is a unity, the thought of which does not exclude, but rather is correlative with, a knowledge of the differences.

In this point of view the Platonic view of science, as a search for unity and the universal, and the Aristotelian view of it as a search for difference and the particular, are but opposite sides of the shield of knowledge, which cannot be separated from each other. Now the defect of Comte's general description of the progress of science is, that he has chosen to look solely at one side of the shield, and to regard it merely as a movement of specification ; and the consequence is, that in the sequel he is obliged continually to correct himself, and to observe in particular cases that it involves also a movement of generalization. Mr. Spencer sees both sides, and therefore progress is for him a movement at once of differentiation and integration ; yet in his criticism of Comte, and in his " First Principles," there are passages in which he seems to confuse the universal of science with a mere abstraction or logical genus, and to overlook the essential correlativity and interdependence of the two opposite movements of thought.* The defects of both writers, however,

* Mr. Spencer, it may be remarked, takes, like Comte, a *negative* view of the progress of religion, and to him,

lie mainly on the metaphysical side ; in their analysis of the idea of development more than in their application of it. And it is the power and fertility of resource with which they apply it to life and history, which gives them, and especially which gives Comte, a claim to an important place among modern philosophical writers.

In this chapter I have tried to trace to their origin Comte's ideas of social and intellectual development, and to examine the motives which led him to reject theology and metaphysics, as legitimate forms of science. In the following chapter I shall go on to consider more carefully the subjective synthesis by which he would supply their place.

therefore, the last religion is the worship of the Unknown, and, indeed, of the Unknowable. But Comte practically retracts this view when he makes the worship of Humanity the last form of religion.

CHAPTER III.

THE POSITIVE OR CONSTRUCTIVE SIDE OF COMTE'S
PHILOSOPHY—HIS SUBSTITUTES FOR METAPHYSIC
AND THEOLOGY.

His recognition of the need of substitutes for Theology and Meta-
physic—His assertion that his philosophy is relative and subjec-
tive—Double meaning of the relativity of knowledge as involving
the assertion or the denial of real or absolute knowledge—
Collision of Comte's earlier and later views on this point—
Comte's subjective synthesis not subjective in the sense of Indi-
vidualism, nor yet in the sense that a conscious subject is im-
plied in all objects—His compromise between these opposite
theories—His doctrine that man sees the world in ordine ad
hominem but not in ordine ad universum—Impossibility
of separating nature from man or of criticising the whole
system to which man belongs—Defects of Comte's religion
according to his own idea of religion—Schisms in the school of
Comte.

IN the preceding chapter I have tried to explain
how Comte was led to treat Metaphysics and
Theology as merely transitional forms of human
thought, and to show that this view not only involves a false conception of their nature, but also

necessitates an entire misrepresentation of the course of their historical development. To regard the history of Metaphysics and Theology as a purely *negative* process, by which the first concrete fulness of religious conceptions was gradually attenuated till nothing remained but the bare abstract idea of Nature, and, on the other hand, to think of the history of science as the corresponding *positive* process, by which the mind of man advanced from the general to the special, from the investigation of the simplest numerical and spatial relations of things to the knowledge of the complex social nature of man—this is a view of man's intellectual history, recommended by its simplicity and clearness, as well as by its correspondence with the most popular philosophy of the present time. But, as we have seen, it involves a one-sided conception of the movement of human thought in its scientific, and still more in its theological and metaphysical, aspects. Comte himself enables us to see that his first description of the history of science is incomplete, if not misleading; and that its movement is towards greater generality as well as towards more definite specification. Now, as Metaphysic is only the clearest

H

form of self-consciousness, and as man's consciousness of himself deepens and widens with his consciousness of the objective world, we might expect to find that Metaphysic also develops at once
towards the universal and towards the particular;
and when we look at the facts of the history of
Philosophy we find this expectation amply realized.
Nor is it otherwise with religion—which is to the
heart and the imaginative intuitions of man what
philosophy is to his self-conscious intelligence ; for
the latest religion is at once the deepest and the
richest, the most complex and the most universal.

Need of sub-stitutes for metaphysic and theo-logy. We cannot, however, give a completely satisfactory answer to Comte's criticism of Metaphysics
and Theology without considering more fully the
substitutes which he would put in their place.
For Comte is not simply an Agnostic; he does not
deny the reality of the wants which Metaphysics
and Theology have hitherto striven to satisfy; nor
does he hold that these wants are, by the nature
of things and of the human intelligence, for ever
precluded from satisfaction.   He does not, like
some modern writers, reduce philosophy into a
consciousness of the limits of the human mind,
and religion into a vague awe of the Unknowable.

On the contrary, he holds that Positivism for the first time supplies complete satisfaction to all the tendencies of the many-sided nature of man, whereas all earlier systems had been obliged to purchase one kind of culture at the expense of another,—to gratify the affections by the sacrifice of intellectual freedom, or to cultivate the intelligence to the neglect of the claims of the heart. To the Metaphysician he grants the necessity of a systematizing of knowledge in relation to one general principle, which shall furnish at once its first presupposition and its end. To the Theologian he grants that that inner harmony with self and with the world, which we call religion, can only be secured by a firm belief and trust in some " Grand Être " who transcends and comprehends our narrow individuality, "in whom we live, and move, and have our being." But while (in opposition to the tendencies of that scientific empiricism, to which the name of Positivism is usually given) Comte thus recognizes those claims of the intelligence and of the heart for which Philosophy and Theology had tried to provide, he still adopts as his own the empiricist condemnation of both, and seeks to show that, on the basis of empiricism itself, we may secure the complete satisfaction of all our spiritual wants. It is to this claim of Comte, to occupy in the name of Science the place from which Theology and Metaphysics have been expelled, that we must now direct our attention.

Distinctions of subjective and objective, relative and absolute. synthesis

The contrast which Comte draws between his own philosophy and religion, and those of his predecessors, is expressed in the words " relative " and " subjective." His purpose, he tells us, is a " subjective synthesis," while his predecessors had aimed at an " objective synthesis " —*i.e., they* had endeavoured to comprehend the world in itself, by carrying its phenomena back to an objective principle to which they are all equally related, and of which they are all the manifestations; while *he* is content to take his stand on the subjective unity of the human race, a unity which has grown out of the conscious or unconscious co-operation of all past generations, and which now manifests itself in the love and reverence of men for each other, and for the *Grand Être,* Humanity, that comprehends them all.* For the existence of *this*

* I need not do more than refer to Comte's view of

Great Being is a fact which we can empirically verify, although we are totally unable to discover the meaning of that wider objective fatality, to which ultimately the fortunes and life of mankind are subjected. Again, Comte contrasts his own philosophy with that of his predecessors, as " relative " with " absolute." By this he means that Positivism does not seek to base itself on absolute knowledge, *i.e.*, on that knowledge of noumenal causes which was claimed by metaphysic, but merely on a knowledge of the laws of phenomena, and that, therefore, the only centre to which our knowledge can be referred and by reference to which it can be organized is the relative centre of Humanity and not the real or absolute centre of the universe. Comte also often uses the word " relative " in a slightly modified sense to indicate that his philosophy takes due account of all the various conditions under which humanity progresses towards its ideal, and does not seek to set up an absolute standard of perfection without reference to the necessary limitations of each stage of development. Now, as it is always best

Humanity as " incorporating " only its *best* members with itself. Something will be said of this below.

to criticize a writer by reference to his own principles and aims, I shall attempt to show that the main errors of Comte arise from his being not " subjective," not " relative " enough, even in the sense which he himself gives to these words. (He is not " subjective " enough ; for in the development of his theory he admits a kind of separation between thought and existence, which a logical development of his own principles must have led him to reject.   And he is not " relative " enough ; for he starts from philosophical principles which involve the denial of any necessary connection between man and the world, and even between the different elements in the nature of man, and he ends with a religion in which poetry is divorced from truth, and truth from poetry.)

Ambiguity in the idea of relativity.   In the first place, however, it is necessary to clear up a certain ambiguity as to the idea of relativity.   It is a commonplace of the sensationalist and empiricist school at the present day, that we are confined to the knowledge of phenomena, and cannot rise to the knowledge of noumena, or things in themselves.   Comte usually expresses this idea by saying that science is limited to the investigation of the laws of phenomena, and that it was the error of Theology and Metaphysics to seek to determine their causes. When, however, we try to ascertain the exact force of this opposition, we find that it may have two distinct meanings. For it is one thing to say, that Theology and Metaphysics gave false answers to a legitimate question, which was afterwards more correctly answered by science; and it is quite another thing to say that they attempted to answer a question different from the question of science, and which it is beyond the powers of the human mind to answer. Now, Comte sometimes speaks as if the error of the Theologians were simply that they sought to explain all phenomena by regarding them as the expressions of divine wills and intelligences analogous to our own; and as if the error of the Metaphysicians were simply that they repeated this explanation in a more irrational form, substituting personified abstractions for Gods. At other times, he speaks as if the error of Theology and Metaphysics were that they attempted to determine the real nature of things, which can be known by us only in their phenomena. On the former view, Theology and Metaphysics are provisional hypotheses, in relation to the objects of experience, which disappear when it is discovered that many of these objects, which were at first assumed to be like man, are in many ways unlike him. On the latter view, they are pretended sciences, which do not relate to the phenomenal objects of experience at all, but to certain realities, supposed to be beneath or behind them. When we disentangle these two different views from each other, we find that they do not rest on the same logical basis, and that they do not by any means imply each other. The former view implies only that our ideas of the world are confused and imperfect, and require to be continually corrected by fresh thought and experience. The latter implies that there are certain objects other than phenomena, the existence of which we know, but the nature of which we gradually discover ourselves to be incapable of determining. It implies, in fact, that our intelligence can discern its own limits, or, what is the same thing, can know that there is something beyond those limits. Now while, with certain modifications we might not hesitate to grant the truth of the former of these doctrines, we should require some proof of the latter, or even of its logical possibility. For by it we are brought face to face with the difficulty of conceiving how we should be able to ask questions, which—not from external circumstances, but from the essential nature of our intelligence—are altogether unanswerable, and which therefore, we can say with certainty, we shall never be able to answer. This, which Mr. Spencer attempts to prove—by very inadequate reasonings as it seems to me—Comte assumes without any proof at all. Hence, while he pretends to renounce metaphysics, he has committed himself to one of the most indefensible of all metaphysical positions. For the assertion that we know only phenomena, has no meaning except in reference to the doctrine that there are, or can by us be conceived to be, *things in themselves—i.e.*, things unrelated to thought; and that, while we know them to exist, we cannot know what they are. Now this dogma is simply the scholastic realism, or what Comte calls metaphysics, in its most abstract and irrational form. It is a residuum of bad metaphysics, which, by a natural nemesis, seems almost invariably to haunt the minds of those writers who think they have renounced metaphysics altogether.

Idealistic view of the relativity of knowledge.   The authority of Kant is often quoted in support of the doctrine of the existence of things in themselves: indeed, it seems to be the doctrine which is most generally associated with his name. But, in spite of some ambiguities, Kant was precisely the writer who, by the general direction and tendency of his thought, did most to free modern speculation from such an illusion. For it was his main aim and purpose to show that the determination of objects as such, is possible only in relation to the unity of apperception, or, in other words, of self-consciousness, and by means of certain universal principles of thought which he calls the Categories. Kant, indeed, says that the objects thus known are merely phenomena, and that things in themselves are unknowable. But even things in themselves are not, in his view, altogether out of relation to consciousness. They are thinkable, though they are not knowable; we have a consciousness of them through the ideas of reason, though they are not objects of experience; and our moral life, bringing with it a consciousness of freedom, turns the thought of them into a conviction of their reality. Further, the later German phil-

osophers, who sought to develop the principles
of Kant to further issues, and to clear away the
inconsistencies of his first expression and application of them, found it necessary to bridge over
the gulf, which Kant had left, between faith and
reason, between noumena and phenomena. Ac-
cordingly we find them insisting upon the
correlation between object and subject, and
pointing out that, if this correlation be taken
strictly, it is a false abstraction to speak at all
of things in themselves which are not relative
to thought, or of a noumenon which is a mere
negation of the phenomenal. There can be no
absolute opposite or negative of that unity of
thought and being, which is presupposed in all
knowledge and experience, and even to speak of
its existence is to use words without meaning.
As Heine says, " The distinction of objects into
phenomena and noumena, *i.e.*, into things that
for us exist, and things that for us do not exist,
is an Irish bull in philosophy." Comte sometimes, especially in the *Politique Positive*, comes
near to the perception of this truth, but his full
apprehension of it is prevented by the presuppositions from which he started, and from which he

could never completely free himself. Thus, in a passage quoted in the previous chapter,* Comte's idea seems to be that the images of things— individual objects as such—are immediately given in sense ; that the mind reacts, in the processes of abstraction and generalization, to raise perception into knowledge ; and that this knowledge, just because of its generality, is sub- jective or relative knowledge. Now this seems to be only a revival of Locke's view that general ideas are necessarily fictitious, because they are the "work of the mind." Yet, in the same paragraph Comte goes on to speak as if the one defect of our knowledge, which prevents it from being adequate to reality, were that our point of view is not *quite* universal, and that we are incapable of *entirely* freeing it

---

* In Pol. Pos. i. 439, Comte seems to come still nearer to the Kantian principle that all existence is existence for a conscious self, but (1) he confounds this principle with the idea that there is an action and reaction between sub- ject and object, which are identified with the organism and the environment respectively ; and (2) he does not draw the necessary inference that the thing in itself is a fiction of abstract thought, or, in other words, that there is no meaning whatever in speaking of an existence which is not relative to the thinking self. Cf. Pol. Pos. iii., p. 18 seq.

from what is subjective. By comparing our
views with those of other men, we can rise above
individual and national prejudices, but we cannot
free our views from those *idola tribus*, which are
common to the whole human race, because we
are unable to establish any satisfactory communication with the animals. Whatever may
be thought of the last suggestion, the passage at
least shows a view of the hindrances to knowledge
which is not consistent with any absolute division between phenomena and noumena. For, if
man can escape from the necessity of viewing
things *in ordine ad individuum, i.e.,* in relation to
his individual self, he is at least on the way
towards regarding them *in ordine ad universum.*
This point, however, will be considered below,
when we come to treat more directly of the
sense in which Comte's synthesis is "subjective."
Here we need only call attention to the difference of this view from that which is suggested
by other passages (especially in his exposition of
the "law of the three stages") in which the knowledge of relations of phenomena is contrasted with
the knowledge of causes. From such passages we
should gather that causes belong to an order of

reality, which is absolutely hidden from us, and to the knowledge of which all our acquaintance with phenomena does not enable us to make any approximation.

The truth seems to be that the absolute distinction of phenomena and noumena—resting as it does on an irrational separation between thought and being—is tenable only from the point of view of a philosophy which regards the individual as the only reality, and the universal as a name or an abstraction. From the point of view of Individualism, it was natural and even necessary for Comte to assail a metaphysic which claimed to apprehend a reality beyond and beneath the phenomenal individuals and their external relations to each other, and which found in this reality the *vera causa* of all phenomenal existence. It was natural for him to maintain that such reality is unknowable for us, and that the general terms which seem to express it are mere collective names for individuals, or, at best, abstract ideas of elements common to many individuals.

But when Comte had so far changed his point of view as to hold that " man is a mere abstraction,

The noumenal, or thing in itself, is really the universal,

and, therefore, can be known.

and that there is nothing real but humanity," he had lost the right to use such language. He had seen that the individual is an abstraction, and he was even in danger of forgetting that the mere universal is an abstraction also. Now modern metaphysic, by showing the relativity of objects to a thinking subject, has banished the idea of real entities, or things in themselves, lying behind and beyond the phenomena; and, at the same time and by the same process of reasoning, it has proved that the individual cannot be separated from the universal, any more than the universal can be separated from the individual. In other words, it has proved that the world cannot be conceived in the spirit of abstract nominalism as a collection of individual objects and events, related *merely* as similar or dissimilar, or co-existent or successive, any more than it can be conceived in the spirit of scholastic realism, as a mere phenomenal appearance of certain noumenal substances, which correspond to general terms. From this point of view, the universal is at once a law and a cause; for it is a principle of unity, which manifests itself in the differences of particulars, and through their relations binds them into one individual whole. If Comte had realized the meaning of the categories by which he was really guided, he must have altered his whole conception of the relation of metaphysic to positive science. For it was his own best achievement to apply this idea of the unity of the universal and particular to one great department of science. It was to show that society, whether in the form of the family, of the nation, or of humanity, is *not* merely a collection of similar individuals, but a unity of organically related members; and that its development is *not* merely a succession of events, but the evolution of one life which remains identical with itself through all its changes. And in this he was not refuting metaphysic, but following directly in the course of the great metaphysicians of the preceding generation. It might, indeed, be shown, that none of the greatest names in philosophy—not Plato or Aristotle, not Spinoza or Leibnitz—was, strictly speaking, either a scholastic realist or a scholastic nominalist, though in all before Kant there were tendencies to one or other of these extremes. But the idealistic movement that took its origin with Kant—and which Comte should have criticized, if his criticism on metaphysic was to be, according to his own frequent phrase, "on the level of his age"—had set before itself as its distinctive purpose and aim, to transcend this opposition. In that philosophy Comte would have found just what he wanted—a way of asserting the reality of the universal, which should not involve the denial of the reality of the individual. For want of this principle, the end of his system comes into contradiction with its beginning. For while Comte begins with a vehement denial of the universal as existent in itself,—a denial which is expressed in the individualistic language of the school of Locke,—he ends with an equally vehement assertion of the social universal against the individualism of Rousseau. And his "subjective synthesis," even its latest form, is embarrassed by hesitations and inconsistencies, which are due mainly to his inability to shake himself free from that implicit nominalism with which he had started.

It is to this last point that we must now direct our attention. What does Comte mean

His subjective synthesis is not Sensationalism.

I

by saying that the ultimate synthesis of knowledge is "not objective but subjective"?   If we
took the words in their most natural meaning,
we should be led to suppose that Comte held
that theory of subjective individualism, which
was the logical result of Berkeley's so-called
idealism, and the basis of the scepticism of
Hume.   Among later writers this theory has
been most fully expressed in some of the works
of J. S. Mill, and it is still offered by Mr.
Spencer and Professor Huxley as one of the two
alternative theories (the other being materialism)
between which philosophy must for ever fluctu-
ate.   According to this view, the individual
directly knows nothing except the states of his
own subjectivity; or, if he seems to know anything else, it is through a process of association,
the result of which can never be verified, seeing
that no one can go beyond the bounds of his
own consciousness.   Now it is obvious that, if
this be the truth, "the subjective" and "the
individual" go together and imply each other;
for, if we cannot transcend our own individuality,
so as to apprehend other things, or come into
communication with other beings, then we must

live a purely subjective life. And if, on the other hand, it can be shown that we know other things and beings as directly and immediately as we know ourselves, then our subjectivity is no longer a limit to us, but a "subjective synthesis" may be at the same time "objective." Now, it was one of the principal results of the German idealism to show that this latter view was the true one, and that thought is not merely a state of the individual subject as such. To speak of the consciousness of the individual as limited to the apprehension of his subjective states, is, indeed the reverse of the truth; for the consciousness of self implies the consciousness of the not-self, and grows with it, and by means of it. We are "a part of all that we have known," and all that we have known is a part of us. Our life widens with our world, and is indeed the same thing from an opposite point of view. When we realize this correlativity of subject and object in knowledge, we can no longer contemplate a thinking being as merely one individual among the other individuals of the world. We are forced to recognize that the consciousness of self lifts him to a universal or central point of view,

—a point of view which is central, not merely in relation to his own feelings and states, but central also in relation to the objective world. The being who knows himself as an individual is, for that very reason, not merely individual; he can know a reality, which is not merely that of his own subjective states or sensations, and he can identify himself with an end, which is not merely his own expected pleasure. The possibility of an intellectual life for us, indeed, lies just in this, that we can regard—nay, that to a certain extent we cannot *but* regard—our own individuality from an "objective" point of view, —a point of view in which *it* has no more importance than other individualities; or in which, at least, all its importance is derived from its relation to the whole of which it is a part. And the poet who said,—

> "Unless above himself he can
> Exalt himself, how mean a thing is man!"

had truly discerned that moral life also is dependent on the transformation of man's individuality by this universal consciousness with which it is linked and bound up.

Now this view of self-consciousness, as objective Nor yet is it idealism. in spite of its subjectivity, universal in spite of its individuality, necessarily leads to a conception of man, not merely as *one* of the many existences in the manifold universe, but as *the* existence in which all the others are summed up, and through which they are to be explained. On one side of his being, indeed, we must regard him as a " part of this partial world," * and, in this point of view, we can understand his life only in relation to the other things and beings which limit him on every side. Nay, as he is the most complex and dependent of existences, we can only rise to a satisfactory knowledge of him, *after* we have laid a basis for this knowledge, in the study of the simpler phenomena of the organic and inorganic world. But, on the other hand, the possibility of all this objective science—of the knowledge by man of that which is not man—lies in this, that he is not merely part of the whole,—not merely the most complex existence in the world,—but that the universal principle, the principle which gives unity to the world, manifests itself in him. It is because, as has been said,

* Cf. Green's Introduction to Hume's Works, § 152.

"Nature becomes conscious of itself in man," that man in his turn can read the open secret of Nature. (In spelling out the meaning of nature and history, he is taking the true way, and indeed the only way, to the knowledge of himself; but this knowledge would be to him impossible, if the self-consciousness that makes him man were not also the principle of unity in the objective world.) Comte himself has an obscure perception of this truth when he says that, "strictly speaking there is no phenomenon within our experience which is not in the truest sense human; and that, not merely because it is man that takes cognizance of it, but also because, from a purely objective point of view, man sums up in himself all the laws of the world, as the ancients truly felt."* If Comte had only brought together the subjective and the objective unity— the unity of knowledge, and the unity of exist- ence—both of which he here finds in man, and if he had recognized the necessary relation of the two, he would have reproduced the highest lesson of German idealism. For that lesson is that the subjective unity, the unity of self-

* Pol. Pos. iv. 181 ; Transl. 161.

consciousness, which is presupposed in all knowledge or experience of the world, must at the
same time be regarded as the objective principle
of its existence. The *macrocosm,* to use an
ancient conception, of which Comte somewhere
speaks with approval, can be comprehensible
only to the *microcosm,* which finds in the great
world the means of understanding itself, just
because in another way it has in itself the
key for the understanding of the world. Man
can know that which is not himself, because
from another point of view there is nothing in
which he does not, or may not, find himself.

It follows from this that the last science, the
science of man, in so far as it is also the
science of mind, cannot merely be built upon
and added to the physical and natural sciences,
but must react upon them and transform them.
For, though the knowledge of man presupposes
the knowledge of nature, yet, on the other hand,
the knowledge of nature which we get, when we
abstract from it its relation to man, is imperfect
and incomplete. The true idea of nature cannot
be attained except when it is viewed in relation
to that being who is at once its culmination and

For idealism
does not
oppose the
subjective
to the
objective.

its explanation.   Or, to put this in another point
of view, the intelligence which appears in man is
presupposed in every object of the intelligible
world.   Self-consciousness is not, therefore, an
episodic appearance in a world, which is unpre-
pared for it, and which might exist, or be understood, without it.   It is the revelation of the
meaning of all that went before.   What Dr.
Tyndall has stated not long since as the modern
view of Materialism, that matter contains in
itself "the promise and the potency" of life and
even of mind, may be willingly accepted as an
expression of their own doctrine by Idealists;
for the converse of this proposition is, that mind
is the "realization," and therefore the only key
to the ultimate nature, of matter.   Hence all
the sciences which treat of the mathematical,
physical, chemical, and vital relations of things,
must be regarded as hypothetical and based
upon abstraction; for thought, spirit, mind, is
implied in all such relations, nor can a complete
or adequate conception of them be attained,
until we have regarded the self-consciousness
that makes us men as, in this point of view,
not only the last, but also the first, not merely

the end, but also the beginning of nature. In this sense the analytic separation of the sciences from each other and from thought must be modified and corrected in a final synthesis, which will indeed be "subjective," in so far as it brings into view the unity of the subject presupposed in all knowledge. But to one who has understood the full meaning of the process, this "subjective synthesis" will also be objective; and, indeed, it alone will be able to vindicate, while it explains, the limited objectivity of the other sciences.

Now it is Comte's merit that he altogether repudiates that false subjective synthesis, which was the natural result of the principles of Locke and Berkeley. Rejecting the doctrine that what we know immediately is only the states of our own consciousness, he takes his stand at an objective point of view, and arranges the sciences in an objective order, which begins with the inorganic world, and ends with man as the most complex of all existences. On the other hand, it is also his merit that he sees the necessity of that true "subjective synthesis" which arises from the reaction of the last science, the science of

He ends, therefore, in a compromise.

man, upon those that went before it; or, in other words, from the perception that man is not merely the end, but also in a sense the beginning of nature. But this ultimate correction and re-organization of science from a subjective point of view appears in Comte in a distorted and imperfect form, in a form that leaves " subjective " and "objective " synthesis still opposed to each other, or only gives room for an artificial or external reconciliation between them. For Comte (in spite of all he says of relativity) does not clearly recognize the subjectivity implied in our first objective knowledge of the world;* and, hence, when he introduces the subjective side of that knowledge, he seems to be starting from a new and independent point of view, and not simply to be bringing into clear consciousness what was presupposed in the previous movement of thought. In other words, the subjective synthesis of Comte does not arise from a perception that the subjectivity of men is universal, and therefore objective. On the contrary, he denies the possibility of discovering any principle of unity in the objective world, and maintains that

* Pol. Pos. i. 420.

the objective sciences, when left to themselves, tend towards the "divagations indéfinies" of a wayward and lawless curiosity. Hence the principle of unity, which is necessary to bring order and system into our knowledge, must be imported into these sciences from without. On this view, we can organize knowledge only in reference to a subjective principle supplied by the altruistic affections,—affections which bind men together so as to make all humanity through all space and time into one great organism, and which thus supply a definite end and aim to all the intellectual, as well as to all the active, energies of the individual. This subjective principle, in Comte's view, has been the unconscious stimulus of all the efforts of the social and intellectual leaders of men in the past; it has been the source of all that organized co-operation of families and nations on which man's physical and moral progress has depended. Positivism has only to make it into the direct aim and conscious purpose of human endeavour, and thereby to check that vain and wasteful application of man's limited powers, which has prevailed in the past, especially during the revolutionary period of transition, now coming to an end. Hence Comte condemns, not only the metaphysicians, who search into things altogether out of the reach of man, but also the scientific men, who seek to extend the knowledge of their special subjects indefinitely in every direction suggested by an empty curiosity, without regard to the practical end of all science. The Mathematician, who wastes himself in the discovery of forms and methods which have no relation to the requirements of physics; the Biologist, who speculates on the origin of species, forgetting how little light such inquiries can throw on the development of man; even the Sociologist, who pursues remote investigations into the history of climate and race, " before such studies are made necessary by the practical difficulty of extending the civilization of the West, regenerated by Positivism, to the populations that are less advanced in civilization " — are all brought under the Comtist anathema, as guilty of wasting the small powers of man on questions which are not immediately necessary or useful. " The public and its teachers should always refuse to recognize investigations which do not tend either to determine more precisely the material and physical laws of man's existence, to throw greater light on the modifications which these laws admit, or at least to render the general method of investigation more perfect." " It is necessary that the sciences should in the first instance be studied independently; but this study should in each case be carried only so far as is necessary to enable the intellect to take a solid grasp of the science next above it in the scale, and thus to rise to the systematic study of Humanity, its only permanent field."* On this principle, the priests of Positivism are not to be specialists; nor, indeed, are any of them to devote their lives to scientific investigation alone; except, it may be, a few distorted and unbalanced natures, in whom an abnormal tendency to intellectual pursuits has stunted the growth of the moral sympathies. (To make scientific men renounce the intellectual life as an end in itself, and to direct all their energies to the solution of those problems which seem to have most immediate relation to the improvement of man's estate, is one of the main objects which Comte has in view in restoring the spiritual

* Pol. Pos. i. 370, 383.

power.   A free development of each science for
itself apart from the rest, and a free development of science as a whole, without reference to
action for ends determined by social sympathy,
are equally opposed to the Comtian ideal.   The
world and all objects in it are to be regarded
by the Positivist merely as means, which we
seek to know not for themselves, but only in
order that we may use them for a predetermined
end.   For, according to Comte, the energies of
the intelligence run to waste except when they
are directed by an *esprit d'ensemble*, and the only
totality, with reference to which such systematic
direction is possible, is the " subjective " totality
of humanity.

Comte
admits a
principle in
man which
is not merely
individual.

I have already indicated to some extent the
grounds on which I would criticize this theory
of " subjective synthesis."   It implies, for one
thing, that there is no natural convergence of
the sciences, due to the unity of the parts of
the intelligible world with each other and with
the intelligence ; but that the synthesis of knowledge is artificial, and forced upon it from without.   Man, in Comte's point of view, is not a
microcosm, who finds himself again in the *macro-*

cosm. He is like a stranger in a foreign country, who seeks to arm himself with such fragments of knowledge about it as are necessary for his protection and his own private ends. Yet this statement, without qualification, would not be altogether just to Comte; for, in his view, the individual man *does* find himself in the presence of *one* "object," which is also "subjective,"— of *one* Great Being, whom he has not to treat as an external means to ends of his own, but rather in whom he has to find his own end. The synthesis of knowledge, therefore, is not subjective so far as Sociology and Morals* are concerned, whatever it may be in regard to the other sciences. The unity, in reference to which knowledge is to be organized, is not merely the unity of man's nature as an individual, but rather as a "collective" being (a bad adjective surely to apply to mankind, when they are regarded as "members one of another"). Comte thus repeats the "*homo mensura*" in the sense that Humanity is for each man the measure of all

* The distinction made in the *Politique Positive* between Sociology and Morals, depending as it does on the opposition of the intellect to the heart, will be discussed afterwards.

things (though things in themselves escape all our measuring). We can transcend ourselves so far as to take the point of view of humanity, though not so far as to take the point of view of the objective unity of the world. Nay, it may even be said that we *must so* transcend ourselves, for Comte denies that the individual can separate himself from his race, except by a forced and illegitimate abstraction. "Man, as an individual," he declares, "cannot properly be said to exist except in the too abstract brain of modern metaphysicians;" and the same principle on its ethical side leads him to condemn the doctrine of absolute personal rights, and to say that "individuals should be regarded not as so many distinct beings, but as organs of the one Great Being." According to these principles it would be impossible for us either to know ourselves as men, or to live a life in accordance with our nature, if we were confined within the limits of a purely individual consciousness. Our consciousness of ourselves is essentially social, and the individualistic point of view is the result of a false abstraction, which can never be more than a partial abstraction.

For, strive as we will, we cannot in thought, any more than in reality, isolate the individual from society, without at the same time taking from him all that characterizes him even as an individual. To speak, therefore, of knowing man, except as a member of the family, of the nation, of the race, is irrational. The science of man would be impossible if we were not able to get beyond our individuality, and to look at it, as well as at all other individualities, from the point of view of humanity.

To such a conception of the essentially social nature of man few, at the present day, would object. But a "metaphysician" might wish to carry it a little farther, and to recognize not only the essential relation of man to man, but also the essential relation of man to the universe. If it is a fiction of abstraction to separate the individual from society, is it a less fiction to isolate him from the world in which he lives, and in relation to which all his powers and tendencies have been developed? Can we really apply the idea of organic unity to the life of man without extending it so as in some sense to include also the environment in which that life develops? To ask what

Yet it is not a universal principle.

K

man would have been in a different world is surely as absurd a question as to ask what he would have been had he not lived with his fellow-men. If it be allowed and asserted that the objective or universal point of view is possible, or even necessary, in relation to humanity, there seems to be no good ground for denying that it is possible and necessary in relation to the universe. Once admit that the individual can, and even must, so transcend his own individuality as to regard himself as part of a greater whole and to measure his actions by another standard than his own pleasures and pains, and you are no longer free to reject the possibility of an objective synthesis. If the relativity of man to man makes it impossible to know him except from the point of view of humanity, the relativity of man to the world makes it impossible to know humanity except from the point of view of the unity of the whole. To stop short at the universal of humanity is a mere compromise, which, like many compromises, is less rational than either of the extremes between which it stands. All knowledge implies the universality of thought, *i.e.,* it implies that man, as a thinking being, can, and indeed must, apprehend the world from a subjective, which is also an objective point, of view. For man's consciousness of himself is at the same time a consciousness of the not-self, and of the unity to which both these correlative elements belong. From the dawning of self-consciousness he is thus lifted above his own separate and partial existence as an individual ; he lives a life which is not merely his own life, but the life of the world. He is, and can become more and more completely, the organ of that universal spirit which transcends and includes all things, which

> " Lives through all life, extends to all extent,
>   Spreads undivided, operates unspent."

It is this that makes him capable of science, or morality, or religion ; for in so far as he speaks his own words, or does his own deeds, or thinks his own thoughts, he speaks and acts and thinks folly and evil ; and it is only in so far as he becomes the instrument of some universal power or interest, that his individual action, or thought, or utterance can have any dignity or value. It shows an imperfect apprehension of this truth to say with Comte that Humanity and not God is the universal power in whose service the individual is to find spiritual freedom; and that, therefore, the ultimate synthesis must be subjective and not objective. (For the only philosophical difficulty is to conceive how man can transcend his individual subjectivity at all; and, if *that* is shown to be for him possible, and even necessary, there is no reason whatever to deny that he can and must rise to the knowledge of God, the absolute or objective unity of the world.)

Comte's changing view of the relation of nature to man.

Comte, however, is hindered from recognizing this truth by another class of considerations. In opposition to that external optimistic teleology, which was so common at the end of last century, and at which the Encyclopedists aimed so many blows, he was led in his *Philosophie Positive* to dwell upon the fact that, from the point of view of human happiness, the arrangements of the universe, astronomical, physical, and biological, are anything but perfect. Poetry, indeed, may be allowed to imagine that the powers of nature are the friends of man; but Science, according to Comte, must recognize that the world in which man's lot is cast is far from furnishing the best conceivable sphere for his existence and development; and that it has only become so favourable to his progress as it at present is, by the long "providential action" of man himself. At this point, however, there is a crossing of opposite lines of thought in Comte's philosophy. For it is one of the leading conceptions of the *Politique Positive* that the influence of an external limiting fatality, which forces upon man the surrender of his natural self-will, was the necessary condition of the development of all his higher powers of intelligence and heart. Comte is never weary of showing that the growing preponderance of the altruistic affections, which alone can give unity to human life, is dependent upon the existence of those limits which are put upon the desires of man by the external world. "Without this continual ascendant," he declares, "man's feelings would become vague, his intelligence wanton, and his activity sterile. If this yoke were taken away, the problem of human life would remain insoluble, since altruism could never conquer egoism. But assisted by the supreme fatality, universal love is able habitually to secure that personality should be subordinated to sociality. The sophisms of human pride cannot hinder the positive spirit from recognizing that all revolt springs from egoistic impulses. A forced submission tends indirectly to make altruism prevail by the very fact that it represses egoism. But this moral reaction is supremely efficacious when obedience becomes voluntary, because then sympathy is directly developed, and no jarring emotion any longer hinders us from getting the benefit of our subjection."* From this point of view the external fatality can no longer be called unfriendly, or even indifferent to man; or rather its immediate appearance as his enemy is the condition of its being, in a higher sense, his friend. Kant, in his short treatise on history (with which Comte was acquainted, and which probably had no little influence upon the *Politique Positive*), applies a similar thought to the struggle and competition of mankind with each other. The very selfish rivalry of men, he contends, is in the long run the means

* Synthèse Subjective, p. 16; cf. Pol. Pos. i., p. 414, seq. and above, p. 36.

of developing a higher sociality than could have existed among a race of beings with whom personal feeling was at first less intense. Egoism itself becomes the means of elevating men above egoism. Thus in both cases, conditions which, in the first instance, seemed to be hostile to the intellectual, and still more to the moral, development of man, become, because of the inner reaction which they call forth in his nature, the best means to that development. "Out of the eater comes forth meat; out of the strong sweetness." On such a view it seems a fair criticism to make that it looks very like a proof that those things which seem in the first instance to be evils, and which, indeed, taken by themselves, *are* evils, are the necessary, though negative, conditions of higher good. But a negative condition is still a condition, and the gods are not envious because they refuse man a lower good in order to make him seek one which is higher. No conclusion unfavourable to Optimism, in any high sense of the word, can be founded on the fact that the world is not arranged for the immediate happiness of man, if that immediate happiness would have been

purchased by his moral degradation ; or even if
it would have been less powerful to call forth
the higher energies of his nature. If the
noblest love is a transmuted and transcended
egoism, then even an infinite benevolence would
not seek directly to stop the unlovely and selfish
struggle which darkens and poisons the life of
man on earth. The best kind of optimism—
the optimism, if we may so term it, of the
deepest and tenderest spirits who have called
themselves Christian—has not been based upon
a shallow and imperfect view of the misery,
still less of the moral evil, of man's life. Rather
it has been attained through the clearest perception of both. It has been an Optimism that
" descended into the grave " of human happiness,
and even, if we might so interpret the creed of
Christendom, into the " hell " of human guilt,
that it might rise again " leading captivity
captive." * And Comte, who in his primary
opposition to theology and metaphysics, had
rejected all absolute or theological conceptions
of the world, is led by the natural development
of his thought to find a higher design in the

* Cf. Von Hartmann's *Selbst-zersetzung des Christenthums.*

immediate negation of design, and to extend to the universe that idea of unity which in the first instance he had applied only to humanity But, as he could never quite forget the negations with which he had started, his recognition of this unity was imperfect, and he was ultimately forced to cast upon poetry the office for which science seemed to be inadequate.

The truth to which these inconsistencies of Comte point, is, that all criticism of the whole system of things to which we belong is, from a truly " relative " point of view, irrational.   For the critic, and the standard by which he criticizes, cannot be separated from that system. To criticize things as particulars is not unreasonable, because we can test the particulars by the universal ; but to criticize the general system of which they and we are parts, and by which our development—and of course among other things, the development of our moral standard—is made possible, is to stand on our own heads and to leap off our own shadow.   If, indeed, we could assume an individualistic point of view, if we could isolate ourselves at once from the world which is our only sphere of activity, and from

The irrationality of pessimistic criticism.

the social life of the race which is the source of all our culture, we might then take the pleasures and pains, the feelings that belong to us as sensitive individuals, as a standard by which to criticize the world. But in any other point of view, criticism is possible only as a reference of the individual to the universal, of the part to the whole, of the various elements and phases of the system of things to the idea, which forms the unity of that system and the principle of its development. It has often been pointed out that a logical scepticism cannot be universal, for every intelligible view of things implies an ultimate unity of thought and of existence, of the *esse* and the *intelligi*. Doubt must rest on a basis of certitude, or it will destroy itself. (But it is not less true, though it is less frequently noticed, that all criticism of the world, while it detects evil in particular, implies an ultimate optimism.) For, if such criticism pretends to be more than the utterance of the tastes and wishes of an individual, it must claim to be the expression of an objective principle—a principle which, in spite of all appearances to the contrary, is realizing itself in the world. If, as Hegel said,

the "history of the world is the judgment of the
world," then, conversely, every true moral judgment is an anticipation of history: it is a discovery
of the hidden forces that are already working
out their triumph in the world, even by means
of that which seems most to oppose them : it is a
prophetic sympathy with the "spirit of the years
to come," which is "yearning to mix itself with
life." It is this objective character which often
makes the words of genius carry with them such
weight and power. "He spake as one having
authority and not as the scribes," could be truly
said only of one, whose speech was like some
natural force in its independence of merely individual and of temporary influences. On the other
hand, it is the limited and subjective character
of many of the ordinary moral judgments of men
—of much of their fault-finding with the conditions of existence, the defects of their neighbours,
and the errors and evils of the time—which
makes us treat such judgments with indifference.
We feel that they are in great part the expression
of personal likes and dislikes, though clothing
themselves in the lion's skin of a moral censorship ; and that the only answer which they de-

serve is, that " there is no disputing about tastes."
Much of the superficial pessimism of our day is
the offspring, not of deep sympathy with the real
evils of humanity, but of a weakness of moral
fibre, which might tempt us to cut the knot of
difficulty with the apparently unfeeling words of
St. Paul, " Shall the thing formed say to him who
has formed it, Why hast thou made me thus ? "
But there is another moral judgment than this,
which is not the mere expression of the tastes
and wishes of individuals, but of the inner law
and the necessity of things, or in other words of
the universal spirit of man, which in the long
struggle of development is becoming more and
more clearly conscious of itself and of the law of
the world.   It is only as the organ of this spirit
that the individual can claim to " judge the world";
nor can he make that claim without taking up
the ground of a philosophical optimism, and
acknowledging that the " soul of the world is
just."   For the sentiment or idea of good implied
in such judgment, must either be the last result of
the development of man in the world—in which
case the system of things which conditioned the
result cannot be criticized by it; or it must be

the pure utterance of individual feeling, in which case it has no objective value whatever. To suppose with Comte that it is *objective,* as being something which belongs not to the individual but to the race, yet *subjective,* as being something that belongs to human nature and not to the nature of things in general, is a hopeless attempt to combine in one two inconsistent points of view—the point of view of the philosophy of Locke, by which the individual consciousness is conceived as confined to the apprehension of its own states, and the point of view of modern idealism, according to which the consciousness of the thinking subject, as such, is universal and objective.

At this point it may be useful to look back and to sum up the various contradictions, or let us rather say, the various forms of the same contradiction, which appear and reappear in different parts of the system of Comte. Beginning with the rejection of metaphysics, because it treats universals as real entities, and with the individualistic definition of science as having to determine *only* the successions and resemblances of phenomena, Comte soon has to point out that in sociology and even in biology we have to

Summary of Comte's inconsistencies.

deal with existences whose parts and successive phases are indefinable, except in and through the whole to which they belong. Beginning with objective science, and thus unconsciously assuming that the subjectivity of thought is not inconsistent with the knowledge of objects as such, he ends by asserting that only a " subjective synthesis " is possible. Yet this subjective synthesis is itself objective, for its point of view is determined, not by the sensations and feelings of the individual subject as such, but by the idea of humanity as a corporate unity. Thus the opposition between subject and object reduces itself to a dualism between the world and man. Hence, in place of the worship of God, the absolute unity to which all thought and existence are referred, Comte would substitute the worship of Humanity, " the real author of the benefits for which thanks were formerly given to God." Finally, even this dualistic view of the world is practically withdrawn. For the negative relation of the external fatality to man's immediate wishes, is proved to be instrumental to his ultimate attainment of a still higher good. And, as if this were not enough, poetry is called in to give complete-

ness to the synthetic view of the world, and to
reconcile the two independent sentiments which
must combine in order to produce a religion, submission and love. For, although Comte at first
thinks it sufficient to say that the necessity of
nature is mediated to us by Humanity, yet in
the end he feels that there will be an essential
imperfection in his religious system, if it cannot
identify the ultimate fatality to which we must
submit with the Great Being whom we are to
love and serve. On this point a few additional
remarks may be useful.

Comte defines religion (and we cannot but acknowledge the substantial truth of the definition)
as the concentration of the three altruistic affections—of Reverence towards that which is above
us, Love towards that which helps and sustains us,
and Benevolence towards that which needs our aid.
It is impossible to give the highest unity to the
inward and outward life of man, except by devotion to a Being in relation to whom these three
affections are identified. Nor can it be denied that
a faith, which has more or less perfectly fulfilled
these conditions, has been the mainspring of human life in all those periods of history in which

Defects of Comte's religion according to his own idea of it.

man has shown the highest powers of his spirit.
" The deepest, nay, the one theme of the world's
history," says Goethe, " to which all others are
subordinate, is the conflict of faith and unbelief.
The epochs in which faith, in whatever form it
may be, prevails, are the marked epochs of
human history, full of heart-stirring memories,
and of substantial gains for all after-times.   On
the other hand, the epochs in which unbelief, in
whatever form it may be, gains its unhappy
victories, even when for the moment they put
on a semblance of glory and success, inevitably
sink into insignificance in the eyes of a posterity
which will not waste its thoughts on things
barren and unfruitful."   The tenderest harmo-
nies of affection, the highest achievements of
passionate energy, the deepest glances of insight
into men and things, the greatest powers of
inspired utterance, cannot be reached except
by minds which are consciously at one with
themselves and with the law of the universe; and
this *oneness* is what we call a religion.   Man can
do his best work only when he feels that he is
the organ or instrument of a power or spirit
which is universal, and therefore irresistible; which

embraces and subordinates even that which seems to resist it. Whether such a faith in its widest sense is still possible to man, or whether Christianity is the last vanishing form of it, and we have now to look about for such substitute for it as may still be within our reach, may be a question. But it can scarcely be questioned, that the Comtist worship of Humanity is only such a substitute, and not the thing itself. Religion, as Comte himself maintains, implies a combination of spontaneity in the worshipper with complete submission and self-surrender to the higher power that controls his life—a combination which can be attained only by one who loves the power to which he submits. But man's life is ultimately limited and determined by cosmical and physical conditions, and in these Comte sees only a fatality which cannot possibly be made the object of love. This difficulty, as we have seen, he tries to escape by showing that the ultimate fatality is mediated to us by Humanity, which, in the long process of its history, has been gradually adapting the sphere of our existence to our physical and moral necessities. He feels, however, that this is only a partial answer, and that the idea of an indifferent

L

outward necessity must be a hindrance to the perfect combination of submission and love. Hence he calls in the aid of poetry to revive the spirit of Fetichism, and to reanimate the dead world by the image of benevolent divine agencies. " The Cultus of Space and of the Earth, completing that of Humanity, makes us see in all that surrounds us the free auxiliaries of Humanity." Comte therefore ends in what some one has called the system of " spiritual book-keeping by double entry," in which imagination is allowed to revive, for practical purposes, the fictions which science has destroyed. In this way poetry has not merely to give sensuous form and life to our creed, by enabling us to see in the part what reason could otherwise find only in the whole ; it has also to supply the defects of a truth which is too hard and painful to satisfy the heart of man. It has to make us forget in our worship the dualism of Nature and Humanity, and to reconcile us to Fate by giving it the semblance of a Providence. It is obvious that poetry is thus made into a kind of deliberate superstition, which stimulates the outflow of religious feeling by hiding from us, for the moment, the realities of our position. But the explanation is that Comte was driven by the ultimate development of his own thought to seek for a kind of unity in the universe, which yet he could not admit without recognizing the error of his original presuppositions. There is a certain irony of fate in the process of unconscious dialectic, by which Comte, the enemy of theology, was led to set up that strange "Trinity in Unity," which is the last word of Positivism.

In Comte's re-construction of religion there seems to be something artificial and factitious, something "subjective," in the bad sense. It is a religion made, so to speak, out of *malice prepense.* "We have derived," he seems to say, "from the experience of our own past and of the past of humanity, a clear idea of what a religion should be: and we also know from the same experience that, without a religion, we cannot have that fulness of spiritual life of which we are capable. Go to, let us make a religion, as nearly corresponding to the definition of religion as modern science will permit. ' Gather up the fragments that remain, that nothing be lost.' God, the Absolute Being, is hidden from us, but Humanity will serve for a ' relative ' or ' subjective ' kind of God : or rather not Hu-

Its artificial character.

manity, but the selected members of the race, whose services entitle them to our recognition, and whom therefore *we* incorporate in the 'Great Being.' And as for the inscrutable fatality that bounds all our views, and on which in the last resort the fate of humanity must depend, to *it* we can but submit, or (since such a separation of submission from love is so far irreligious) we can invoke the powers of imagination to hide it from our eyes. To Humanity, as represented to us by the good and wise of the past, we can present the old offerings of praise and prayer, in a spirit that is perfectly disinterested; for we have no reason to believe that *they* exist except in our memory of them, or that the 'Great Being,' in whom they are incorporated, has any gift to bestow upon us in the future except a similar life in the memory of others. For, after all, the 'Great Being,' who alone makes things work together for our good and whom alone we can love, is not absolute or objective; and of the real Absolute Being or Principle of the Universe, we know nothing, except perhaps that He or It is not what men call *good.*"

A relative religion is no religion.

In the earlier part of this chapter I have tried to show that Comte's view of the limits of knowledge cannot be maintained except on principles which would be fatal to the existence of knowledge altogether; and, on the other hand, that the possibility of a subjective synthesis, such as he demands and supposes himself to have achieved, would involve also the possibility of an objective or absolute synthesis. Here I wish only to point out, that if Comte's general view of things be admitted, religion, according to his own definition of it, is impossible. A "relative" religion is not a religion at all: it is at best a morality, trying to gather to itself some of the emotions which were formerly connected with religious belief. If there is no warrant for the Christian faith which finds God in man, and man in God, which makes us regard the Absolute Being as finding his best name and definition in what we most reverence and love; or, what is the same thing from the other side, makes us see in that growing idea of moral perfection, which is the highest result of human development, the interpretation or revelation of the Absolute; then we must give up the hope of the renewal of religion, and of that harmonious energy to which religion alone can

awake the soul of man.   In this point of view
Mr. Spencer and Comte seem to divide the
elements of the truth between them,   Mr.
Spencer, regarding the Absolute as unknowable,
and perceiving that religion implies a relation
to the Absolute, reduces religion to the bare
feelings of awe and mystery.   Comte, also regarding the Absolute as unknowable, seeks to
find an object nearer home for the emotions
that hitherto have been directed to God.   But
the religion of Mr. Spencer, if it ever could
become a reality, would be a renewal of the
superstitious pantheism of India, the worship
of a power without moral or spiritual attributes.
And the religion of Comte could scarcely become more than a pious aspiration, unless the
poetic license of worship were carried to the
point of self-deception.   Of this Comte seems
to be partially aware, when in his latest works
he insists so strenuously on the theme that
art, rather than science, is the true field for
man's intelligence, and that it is a desirable
and useful thing to allow our minds to dwell
on ideal conceptions, which are beyond the reach
of scientific proof, provided these conceptions are

favourable to the development of altruistic sentiment. " The logic of religion," he declares,
" when freed from scientific empiricism, will not
restrain itself any longer to the domain of hypotheses which are capable of verification, though
these alone were compatible with the Positive
preparation for it. It must in the end find
its completion in the domain, much wider and
not less legitimate, of those conceptions which,
without offending the reason, are peculiarly
suited to develop the feelings. Better adapted
to our moral wants, the institutions of true
Poetry are as harmonious as those of sound
Philosophy with the intellectual conditions of
the relative synthesis. They ought therefore
to obtain as great extension and influence in
our efforts to systematize our thoughts ; and
Positivism permits of their doing so without
any danger of confusion between the two distinct methods of thinking, which it openly
consecrates, the one to reality and the other
to ideality." * Is it possible to express more
clearly a desire to combine the advantages of
believing, with the advantages of disbelieving,

* Synthèse Subjective, p. 40.

in the accordance of objective reality with our
highest feelings and aspirations ?   But a worship
of fictions, confessed as such, is impossible.   Art,
indeed, is kindred with Religion ; and Art, as
Plato said, is " a noble untruth."   This, however,
means only that Art is untrue to the immediate
appearances of things, in order that it may suggest the deeper reality that underlies them.   But,
in Comte's view, the service of imagination is
to supply wants of the heart, which *cannot* be
supplied by reality, either in its superficial or
in its deeper aspect ; it is to nurture our
moral nature on conceptions that are purely
fictitious.   It is not difficult to prophesy that
the schism of the head and the heart thus
introduced must end in the sacrifice either of
the one or of the other ; either in the dogmatic
assertion of the optimism of poetry, or in a
violent recoil from it, which will separate, not
only man from the world, but also the individual
from the race, and which must ultimately reduce
Humanity from an object of worship into a
purely moral ideal.   For religion, as Comte
himself rightly saw, cannot exist except where
thought and feeling, intelligence and heart, are

harmonized, in a consciousness of the highest *subjective ideal,* as being at the same time the ultimate *objective reality.* What, indeed, is the use of religion, if it does not plant our feet upon the "Rock of Ages," but leaves us still on the "sandbank" of the contingent and the temporal? "All the nations," says Hegel, "have felt that the religious consciousness was that in which they possessed *truth,* and it is for this reason that they have ever regarded it as that which gives dignity and consecrated joy to their lives. All that awakes doubt and anguish, all sorrow and care, all the limited interests of finitude, the religious spirit leaves behind on the sandbank of time. And as, on the highest top of a mountain, removed from definite view of the earth below, we peacefully overlook all the limitations of the landscape and the world, so, to the spiritual eye of man in this pure region, the hardness of immediate reality dissolves into a semblance, and its shadows, differences, and lights are softened to eternal peace by the beams of the spiritual sun." If we cannot any longer have this consciousness of things *sub specie æternitatis,*—in that highest truth and unity in which all difficulties and dissonances are lost,—without self-deception, it would be better for us to forswear it altogether than to connect our highest feelings with a poetic illusion.

Schisms in the school of Comte. It is a natural question to ask whether and how far the history of Comte's philosophy illustrates any of the difficulties and contradictions which we have found in the writings of its author. The first schism in the ranks of those who are commonly called Positivists was that which is connected in France with the name of Littré, perhaps the most distinguished of Comte's disciples ; and in England, with the names of Mill and Lewes—who, however, were never, strictly speaking, his disciples at all. These writers broke away from Comte, whenever Comte decidedly broke away from the individualistic philosophy of the last century. In their eyes Comte's great achievements were the law of the three stages of mental development and the arrangement of the sciences ; and if they accepted his sociological speculations—even those which appear in his first great work—it was with many reserves.

Mill regards Comte's continual denunciation of metaphysics as objectionable, so soon as he finds it to be directed against the individualists * as well as against the scholastic realists; and he thinks Comte's " inordinate demand for unity and systematization " only an instance of " an original mental twist very common in French writers, and by which Comte was distinguished above them all."† Littré finds little to object to in Comte's first great work, and is not unwilling to admit that the "individual man is an abstraction, and that there is nothing real but humanity;" but he recoils when Comte begins to speak of the "Great Being," and to change his philosophy into a religion. Both attack the "subjective synthesis" as a new variety of metaphysics, seeing clearly that, as Comte states it, it involves a desertion of the point of view of science; and neither of them is able to admit any other point of view from which the subjective unity might itself be seen to be objective.

A less important schism has recently‡ occurred Mr. Congreve and M. Lafitte.

---

* Mill's Comte and Positivism, p. 73.
† Id. p. 140.   ‡ Written in 1879.

within the Positivist Church, or, in other words, among those who accept the system of Comte in its entirety, as a religion no less than as a philosophy. Mr. Congreve, and those who think with him, have broken away from the general body of Positivists under M. Lafitte, who was appointed to be its head, or, at least, its provisional head, after the death of Comte. The difference, however, is one only of policy, and not of principle. "There exists no difference," says Mr. Congreve, " in regard to the doctrine, taken as a whole ; it is only as to the manner of presenting that whole that we are at variance." At the same time this " schism," though, as M. Lafitte says, it is not a " heresy," might easily lead to one, if there be any truth in what has been said above as to the ultimate opposition of poetry and philosophy in the system of Comte. M. Lafitte contends that the Positivist priesthood should, in the first instance at least, seek to address the heart through the intelligence ; "for it is clear that their direct sentimental (or moral) action would want a basis, and could indeed have no serious result, unless general opinion had previously been

modified to a certain degree by Positive teaching."
On the other hand, Mr. Congreve argues that
Positivism must triumph in the first instance,
like Christianity, by a direct "appeal to the
women and the proletaries"; which means
that an effort must be made to influence "the
heart," without waiting for the intelligence; and
that, in the words of Comte himself, the "weapon
of persuasion is to be used in preference to that
of conviction." "What we seek to constitute,"
says Mr. Congreve,* "is a union of the faithful,
a Church in the highest sense of the term, *i.e.*,
a society in which the religious element will
preponderate; will, indeed, be so decisively
and boldly emphasized, as to leave no doubt of
our intentions; a society which can rally to
itself all who feel the need of shelter or support, of the consolation of an active and sym-
pathetic faith. It is thus that we conceive
ourselves bound to commence the preaching of
Humanity, as a principle of union, with the
view of gathering together a solid body, made
up mainly of the women and the populace,

---

* I translate from the French, as I have not seen the
English edition of Mr. Congreve's circular.

which may serve as a foundation for the rest. In this body the order of instructors could find their support (and by an order of instructors I mean naturally a priesthood and priests, and not, what seems to be offered in its place, professors and a professoriate), as, on the other hand, without the stimulating reaction of such an audience, they would want a solid basis as well as a sphere of activity." It would be an impertinence for any one who is not a member of the Positivist Church to say anything on the personal or semi-private questions, which are necessarily involved in such a division as this between those who are otherwise united. But there can be no intrusion in saying, that if Positivism is ever to become an effective Church, it must find some such direct way of addressing the people as Mr. Congreve suggests, without waiting for those who have time to be instructed in the principles of the six or seven sciences of the Positivist system; and Mr. Dix Hutton* has sufficiently shown that

* I have to offer to Mr. Dix Hutton my best thanks for his courtesy in furnishing me with copies of the circulars and letters of himself, of Mr. Congreve, and of

Comte himself would have approved of such a policy. "God hath chosen the weak things of the world to confound the mighty;" and it may be safely said that no great moral or spiritual movement will ever be accomplished, if its leaders wait till they have convinced the mass of the educated classes. The only question which suggests itself to one who has considered the difficulties of the " subjective synthesis " is, whether the appeal made to the heart would not necessarily contain elements which afterwards it would be impossible to justify to the head. For if it were so, "the old quarrel of the poets and the philosophers," of faith and reason, would repeat itself again in the Positivist Church, and it would not be less bitter from the fact that that Church was founded expressly with the design of putting an end to the quarrel altogether.

Can there be a division of the intelligence against the heart, which is not more properly described as division of the intelligence against itself ? This is a question which is inevitably suggested

The heart and the head.

M. Lafitte, on the subject of the division among the Positivists.

by the whole tenor of Comte's later works. In my final chapter I shall say something upon this question, and shall then try to show how Comte's defective answer to it naturally led to other defects in his view of the history of the past, especially of Christianity, and also in his view of the social ideal of the future.

CHAPTER IV.

COMTE'S VIEW OF THE RELATION OF THE INTELLECT
TO THE HEART—ITS EFFECT ON HIS CONCEPTION
OF HISTORY AND OF THE SOCIAL IDEAL.

*The necessity for unity in man's intellectual and moral life—
Nature of the conflict between the intelligence and the heart—
It is really a conflict of intelligence with itself—Criticism of
Comte's doctrine that the intelligence must be subjected to the
heart—Its effect upon his conception of history, especially of
the history of Christianity—The two elements in Christianity,
their conflict and reconciliation in its development—The negative tendencies of mediæval Catholicism and the positive tendencies of the modern era—Comte's imperfect conception of the
Reformation and the Revolution — His restoration of the
mediæval ideal—His general position as a Philosopher.*

IN the last chapter I considered the subjective
synthesis of Comte, or in other words, his attempt
to systematize human knowledge in relation to
the moral life of man. For it is his view, as we
have seen, that science can never yield its highest
fruit to man unless it be systematized—*i.e.,*

M

unless its different parts be connected together and put in their true place as parts of one whole. Scattered lights give no illumination; it is the *esprit d'ensemble*, the general idea in which our knowledge begins and ends, that ultimately determines the scientific value of each special branch of knowledge. But while synthesis is necessary, it is not necessary, according to Comte, that the synthesis should be objective. The error of mankind in the past has been that they supposed themselves able to ascertain the real or objective principle, which gives unity to the world, and able, therefore, to make their system of knowledge an ideal repetition of the system of things without them. Such a system, however, is entirely beyond our reach. The conditions of our lot, and the weakness of our intelligence, make it impossible for us to tell what is the real principle of unity in the world, or even whether such a principle exists. The attempts to discover it, made by Theology and Metaphysics, have been nothing more than elaborate anthropomorphisms, in which men gave to the unknown and unknowable reality a form which was borrowed from their own nature. They saw in the clouds about them an exaggerated and distorted reflection of themselves, and regarded this Brocken spectre as a controlling power whose activity was the source and explanation of everything. Positivism, on the other hand, arises whenever men come to recognize the nature of this illusion, and to confine their ambition to that which is within the limit of their intelligence. All that we can know is the resemblances and successions of phenomena, and not the things in themselves that are their causes; and if we seek to find a principle of unity for these phenomena, we must find it in ourselves and not in them. We must organize knowledge with reference to our own wants, rather than with reference to the nature of things. We must regard everything as a means to an end, which is determined by some inner principle in ourselves—not as if we supposed that the world and all that is in it were made for us, or found its centre in us—but simply because this is the only point of view from which we can systematize knowledge, as it is indeed the only point of view from which we need care to systematize it.

Necessity of
unity and
system.

It may be asked why system is necessary at all, why we should not be content with a fragmentary consciousness of the world, without attempting to gather the dispersed lights of science to one central principle. To critics like J. S. Mill Comte's effort after system seems to be the result of an "original mental twist very common in French thinkers," of "an inordinate desire of unity." "That all perfection consists in unity, Comte apparently considers to be a maxim which no sane man thinks of questioning: it never seems to enter into his conceptions that any one could object *ab initio*, and ask, why this universal systematizing, systematizing, systematizing. Why is it necessary that all human life should point but to one object, and be converted into a system of means to a single end?"* To this Mr. Bridges answers that unity in Comte's sense is "the first and most obvious condition which all moral and religious renovators, of whatever time and country, have by the very nature of their office set themselves to fulfil."† In other words, all moral and spiritual life depends upon the harmony of the

* "Comte and Positivism," p. 140.
† "The Unity of Comte's Life and Doctrine," p. 26.

individual with himself and with the world. A divided life is a life of weakness and misery, nor can life be divided intellectually, without being, or ultimately becoming, divided morally. Such unity, indeed, does not exclude—and in a being like man who is in course of development cannot altogether exclude—difference and even conflict. In the most steadily growing intellectual life there are pauses of difficulty and doubt; in the most continuous moral progress there are conflicts with self and others. But such doubts and difficulties will not greatly weaken or disturb us, so long as they are partial, so long as they do not affect the central principles of thought and action, so long as there is still some fixed faith which reaches beyond the disturbance, some certitude which is untouched by the doubt. If, however, we once lose the consciousness that there is any such principle, or if we try to rest on a principle which we at the same time feel to be inadequate, our spiritual life, in losing its unity or harmony with itself, must at the same time lose its purity and energy. It must become fitful and uncertain, the sport of accidental influences and tendencies; it must lower its moral

and intellectual aims.   This, in Comte's view, is
what we have seen in the past.   The decay of
the old faiths, and of the objective synthesis
based upon them, has emancipated us from many
illusions, but it has, as it were, taken the inspiration out of our lives.   It has made knowledge a
thing for specialists who have lost the sense of
totality, the sense of the value of their particular
studies in relation to the whole ; and it has made
action feeble and wayward by depriving men of
the conviction that there is any great central aim
to be achieved by it.   And these results would
have been still more obvious, were it not that
men are so slow in realizing what is involved
in the change of their beliefs ; were it not that
the habits and sympathies developed by a creed
continue to exist long after the creed itself has
disappeared.   In the long run, however, the
change of man's intellectual attitude in relation
to the world must bring with it a change of
his whole life.   Ceasing to have faith in the
creed which once reconciled him to the world
and bound him to his fellows, he must be
thrown back upon his own mere individuality,
unless he can find another creed of equal or

greater power to inspire and direct his life. And mere individualism is nothing but anarchy. This, indeed, was not seen by those who first expressed the individualistic principle; on the contrary, they seemed to themselves to find in the assertion of individual right, not only an instrument for destroying the old faith and the old social order, but also the principle of a better faith, and the means of reconstructing a better order of life. But to us who have outlived the period when it could be supposed that the destruction of old, involves in itself the construction of new, forms of life and thought, it cannot but be obvious that the principles of private judgment and individual liberty are nothing more than negations. For, as the real problem of our intellectual life is how to rise to a judgment which is more than private judgment, so the real problem of our practical life is how to realize a liberty that is more than individual license. Hence it is that Comte speaks of the last three centuries as a period of the insurrection of the intellect against the heart, an expression by which he means to indicate at once the gain and the loss of

the revolutionary movement: its gain, in so far
as it emancipated the intelligence from superstitious illusions: and its loss, in so far as it
destroyed the faith which was the bond of social
union, without substituting any other faith in
its room. At the same time, this expression
points to a peculiarity of Comte's Psychology,
which affects his whole view of the history,
and especially of the religious history, of man;
and which it is therefore necessary to subject
to a careful examination.

Possibility
of conflict
between
intellect and
heart.Is it possible for the intellect to be in insurrection against the heart ? In the sense already
indicated this is possible. It is possible, in short,
that the moral and intellectual spirit of a belief
may still control the life of one who, so far as his
explicit consciousness is concerned, has renounced
it. Rooted as the individual is in a wider life
than his own, it is often but a small part of himself that he can bring to distinct consciousness.
Further, so little are most men accustomed to
self-analysis, that they are seldom aware what it
is that constitutes the inspiring power of their
beliefs. Generally, at least in the first instance,
they take their creed in gross, without distinguish-

ing between essential and unessential elements.
They confuse, in one general consecration of reverence, the primary principles, which give it its
real spiritual value, and the local and temporary
accidents of the form in which it was first presented to them ; and they are as ready to accept
battle *à l'outrance* for some useless outwork as for
the citadel itself. And, for the same reason, they
are ready to think that the citadel is lost when
the outwork is taken ; to suppose, *e.g.*, that the
spiritual nature of man is a fiction, if he was not
directly made by God out of the dust of the earth,
or that the Christian view of life has ceased to be
true, if a doubt can be thrown on the possibility
of proving miracles. Yet, however little the individual may be able to separate the particulars
which are assailed from the universal with which
they are accidentally connected, his whole nature
must rebel against the sacrifice which logical con-
sistency seems in such a case to demand from
him. It is a painful experience when the first
break is made in the implicit unity of early faith,
and it is painful just in proportion to the depth
of the spiritual consciousness which that faith has
produced in the individual. Unable to separate

that which he is obliged to doubt from that in
which lies the principle of his moral, and even of
his intellectual, life, he is " in a strait betwixt
two "; and no course seems to be open to him
which does not involve the surrender, either of his
intellectual honesty, or of that higher consciousness which alone " makes life worth living." Such
a crisis is commonly described as a division between the heart and the head, because in it the
articulate or conscious logic is generally on the side
of disbelief, while the resisting conviction takes the
form of a feeling, an impulse, an intuition, which
the individual has for himself, but which
he is unable to communicate in the same
force to another.   And, as such feelings and
intuitions of the individual are necessarily
subject to continual variation of intensity and
clearness, so the struggle between doubt and
faith may be long and difficult, the objections,
which at one time seem as nothing, at another
time appearing to be almost irresistible.   Not
seldom the result is a broken life, in which youth
is given to revolt, and the rest of existence to a
faith which vainly strives to be implicit.   There
is, indeed, no final and satisfactory issue from

such an endless internal debate **and conflict, until** the " heart " has **learned to** speak the language of the " head,"—*i.e.,* until the **permanent** principles, which **underlay and** gave strength to faith, have been **brought into the** light of distinct conscious- ness, **and** until it has been discovered how to separate them from the accidents, with which at first they were necessarily **identified.   The hard** labour of distinguishing, in the traditions of **the** past, between the germinative principles, out **of** which the **future must** spring, and those external **forms and adjuncts, which every day is making more incredible, must be undertaken by any one who would** restore the broken unity **of man's life. We** begin our existence under the shadow and in- fluence of a faith which is given to us, as it were, in our sleep ; but in no age, and in this age **less than any other, can man possess spiritual life as** a gift **from the past without reconquering it for himself.**

In this sense, **then, we can** understand how Comte might speak **of an** insurrection of the in- telligence **against the heart, which must be quelled ere the normal state of humanity could be re- stored ; for this would be only another way of**

Real nature of the opposition.

saying that, in the modern conflict of faith and reason, the substantial truth, or at least the most important truth, had, up to Comte's own time, been on the side of the former. In this view, the deep unwillingness of those nourished in the Christian or Catholic faith to yield to the logical battery of the Encyclopædists was not merely the result of an obscurantist hatred of light; it was also in great part due to a more or less definite sense of the moral, if not the intellectual, weakness of the principles which the Encyclopædists maintained. For, while the insurrection was justified in so far as it asserted the claims of the special sciences, it was to be condemned in so far as it involved the denial of all synthesis whatever, and also in so far as it was blind to the elements of truth in the imperfect synthesis of the past. It thus tended to destroy the spirit of totality and the sense of duty (*l'esprit d'ensemble et le sentiment du devoir*).*
It practically denied the existence of any universal principle which could connect the different parts of knowledge with each other, of any general aim which could give unity to the life of man. Its analytic spirit was fatal, not only to the fictions

* Pol. Pos. iii. 499 : Trans. 419.

of theology, but also to that growing consciousness of the solidarity of men of which theology had been the accidental embodiment. The reluctance of religious men to admit the claims of what appeared to be, and, indeed, to a certain extent was, light, was thus due to a more or less distinct perception that their own creed, amid all its partial errors, contained a central truth more important than all the partial truths of science. In clinging to the past they were preserving the germ of the future, and the final victory of science could not come until this germ had been disengaged from the husk of superstition under which it was hidden. Till that was done, the logic of the heart in clinging to its superstitions was better than the logic of the head in rebelling against them. In other words, the implicit reason of faith was wiser than the explicit reason of science.

But this is not all that Comte means. For him the appeal to the heart is not merely the appeal to feelings and intuitions, which are the result of the past development of human intelligence, and especially of the long discipline by which the Christian Church has moulded the modern spirit ; it is an appeal to the altruistic affections, as ori-

Feeling apart from intelligence has no definite content.

ginal or "innate" tendencies in man which are altogether independent of his intelligence. It is not that the reason of man often speaks through his feelings, but that feeling and reason have in themselves different, and even it may be opposite voices. In this sense, the attempt has often been made in modern times to stop the invasions of critical reflection by setting up the heart as an independent authority. From the Lutheran theologian who said, "*Pectus theologum facit*," down to the poet of *In Memoriam*, appeals have constantly been made to the feelings to resist the intrusion of doubt :—

> "If e'er when faith had fall'n asleep,
> 　I heard a voice, 'believe no more' . . .
> A warmth within the breast would melt
> 　The freezing reason's colder part,
> 　And like a man in wrath, the heart
> Stood up and answered, 'I have felt' : "

Such appeals, however, cannot be regarded as otherwise than provisional and self-defensive. "The heart knoweth its own bitterness, and a stranger doth not intermeddle with its joy;" but just for that reason it has no general content or independent authority of its own. Whether the phrase "I feel it" mean little or much, depends upon the

individual who utters it. It may be the concentrated expression of a long life of culture and
discipline, or it may be the loud but empty voice
of untrained passion and prejudice. The "unproved assertions of the wise and experienced,"
as Aristotle tells us, have great value, especially
in ethical matters ; but it is not because they
are unproved assertions, but because we know
that the speakers are wise and experienced.
To appeal to the heart in general, without
saying "*whose* heart," either means nothing,
or it means an appeal to the natural man,
i.e., to man as he is before he has been sophisti-
cated by culture and experience. But of the
natural man, in this sense, nothing can be said.
The farther we go back in the history of the
individual or the race the more imperfect does
their utterance of themselves become ; and
when we reach the beginning, we find that
there is no manifestation or utterance at all.
The natural man of Rousseau was simply an
ideal creation, inspired with that intense and
even morbid consciousness of self and that fixed
resolve to submit to no external law, which were
characteristic of Rousseau himself, and which in

him were the last product and quintessence of
the individualism of the eighteenth century.
The simplicity of this ideal figure is not the
first simplicity of nature, but the simplicity of a
spirit which has returned upon itself and asserted
itself against the world ; a kind of simplicity
which never existed, at least in the same form,
before the great Protestant revolt. The unhistorical character of this idea becomes doubly
evident when we find that, as time goes on,
and the spirit of the age alters, the qualities
of the natural man are also changed. To St.
Simon and Fourier, as to Rousseau, man is good
by nature, and it is bad institutions or bad external influences which are the source of all the
ills that flesh is heir to. But while to the
latter the natural man is a solitary, whose chief
good lies in the preservation of his independence ;
to the former he is essentially social, and what
is wanted for his perfection and happiness is
only to contrive an outward organization in which
his social sympathies shall have free play.
Comte, as we might expect, rises above these
imperfect theories, in so far as he refuses to
attribute all the evils of humanity to its external

circumstances; but he does not free himself from
the essential error which was common to them all,
the error of seeking for the explanation of the
higher life of humanity in the feelings of the
natural man—feelings which are prior to, and
independent of, the exercise of his reason, and
which supply all the possible motives for that
exercise. There are, in his view, two sets of
"innate" feelings or desires, between which
man's life is divided—the egoistic and the altruistic tendencies, each separate from the others
as well as from the intelligence, and having its
"organ" in a separate part of the brain. The
egoistic feelings at first exist in man in far
greater strength than the altruistic; but by the
reaction of circumstances, and the influence of
men upon each other, the latter have in the
past gradually attained to greater power; and
it is the ideal of the future to make their victory
complete. Meanwhile, the intelligence is necessarily the instrument of desire, and its highest
good is to be the instrument of altruistic as
opposed to egoistic desire. For it has at best
only a choice of masters, and the emancipation
of the intelligence from the heart could mean

only its becoming a slave of personal vanity.* Comte's appeal, therefore, is still to the natural man, or rather to one element in him, which, however, as he acknowledges, is never so weak as it is in man's earliest or most natural state.

Hume's view of the relation of reason and passion.

The psychology implied in this theory is substantially that which found its fullest expression in Hume's "Treatise on Human Nature." Hume, with that tendency to bring things to a distinct issue which is his best characteristic, declares boldly that "reason is and ought to be the slave of the passions, and can never pretend to any other office than to serve and obey them." The passions or desires are tendencies of a definite character which exist in man from the first; the awaking intelligence cannot add to their number, or essentially change their nature. It can only take account of what they are, and calculate how best to satisfy them. "We speak not strictly and philosophically when we talk of the combat of reason and passion," for while reason determines what is true and what is false, it sets nothing before us as an end to be pursued and avoided. It does not constitute, and it cannot transform,

* Pol. Pos. i. 421.

the desires, which are given altogether apart from
it: nor is the will anything but the strongest
desire. When we say that reason controls the
passions what we mean is simply that a strong
but calm tendency of our nature, which has
reference to some remote object, overcomes a
violent impulse towards a present delight; but
for intelligence to contend with passion is, strictly
speaking, an impossibility.

The modifications which Comte makes in this
view of motive are comparatively trifling. He
does not, indeed, like Hume, call reason the
slave of the passions; rather he says that
" *l'esprit doit être le ministre du cœur, mais jamais
son esclave;*" but this change of language does
not involve any important modification of Hume's
theory. The intelligence may give the heart
much information about the means whereby it
may attain its ends, but the ends have to be
determined solely by the heart itself. In Comte's
language the intellect is a "slave," when theology
makes it acknowledge the existence of fictitious
supernatural beings whose natures are in accordance with our desires, our hopes or our fears; it
is a "master," when it pursues its inquiries into

the phenomena of the objective world, at the bidding of an errant curiosity, without reference to the well-being of man; it is in its true place as a "servant" when it studies the objective world freely, but only with reference to the end fixed for it by the affections. "*L'univers doit être étudié non pour lui-même, mais pour l'homme, ou plutôt pour l'humanité;*" and this, Comte thinks, will not be done if the intelligence be left to itself, but only if it be made subordinate to the heart. To say, therefore, that the intelligence is not to be a slave but a servant, implies merely that it is to be left free to collect information about the means of satisfying the desires, without having its judgment anticipated by the imagination or the heart; but that, on the other hand, it must be kept strictly to its position as an instrument to an end out of itself. For if it once emancipates itself from the yoke of feeling, it soon becomes altogether lawless, and disperses its efforts in every direction in the satisfaction of a vain curiosity. The intelligence, as the scholastic theologians said, is in itself, or when left to itself, a source of anarchy and confusion; it must be, not indeed the *serva*, but the *ancilla fidei* otherwise it will defeat its own ends. The intellectual life, as such, is an unsocial, even a selfish existence; for, as reason is guided by no definite objective aim derived from itself, it must find its real motive in the satisfaction of personal vanity and self-conceit, whenever it is not subjected to the yoke of the altruistic affections.

This theory (which, as we shall see, underlies Comte's whole conception of history) suggests two questions. It leads us to ask, in the first place, whether the tendencies of the intellectual life are thus dispersive and opposed to the social tendencies: and, secondly, whether the social tendencies in the form which they take with man, are not necessarily determined to be what they are by his intelligence. The former question really resolves itself into another: Is the intelligence of man a mere formal power of apprehending what is presented to it from without, so that, when it is left to itself, it can only lose its way amid the infinite multiplicity of individual objects in the external world; or does it carry within it any synthetic principle, any idea of the whole, by which it can reduce to unity and order the difference and confusion of phenomena?

Are the tendencies of the intellect purely dispersive?

Against Comte's assertion that the natural tendency of the intelligence is to lose itself in difference without end, we might quote the well-known saying of Bacon, that the tendency of the "*intellectus sibi permissus*" is rather towards a premature synthesis. "*Intellectus humanus ex proprietate sua facile supponit majorem ordinem et æqualitatem in rebus quam invenit.*" Surely, if we may speak of tendencies of the intellectual life as separated from the life of feeling, the tendency to unity and the universal belongs to it quite as much as the tendency to difference and the particular; just as in the life of feeling the tendency to isolation and self-assertion against others is combined with the tendency to society and union with others. From the first moment of intellectual life the world is to us a unity; *subjectively* a unity, as all its varied phenomena are gathered up in the consciousness of one self, and *objectively* a unity, as every object and event is conceived as definitely placed in relation to the other objects and events in one space and one time. The development of knowledge is, no doubt, the continual detection of new differences and distinctions in things, but the phenomena which are distinguished from other phenomena are at the same time put in relation to them. Nor can the intelligence find complete satisfaction until this relation is discovered to be necessary, and thus difference passes into unity again. Individual minds, indeed, may be more of the Aristotelian, or more of the Platonist, order, may tend more to divide what at first is presented as unity, or to unite what at first is presented as difference. But it is absurd to talk of either tendency as belonging, more than the other, to the intelligence in itself: seeing that it is as much beyond the powers of thought to conceive of an undifferentiated unity, as to conceive of a chaos of differences without some kind of relation. In this regard, indeed, we may bring Comte as a witness against himself; for, while he declares that the sciences which deal with the inorganic world are mainly analytic in their tendencies, he at the same time maintains that the sciences of Biology, and, still more, of Sociology and Morals, are synthetic, since they deal with objects in which the whole is not a mere aggregation or resultant of the parts, but in which rather the parts can be understood only in and through the whole. Hence it would seem that the dispersive tendencies of science are confined to the lower steps of the scientific scale ; and that the final science admits and necessitates a synthesis, which is not merely subjective, but also objective. For Comte does not hold that we are to regard other men merely as means, or to seek to understand them only so far as is necessary for the gratification of some desire in ourselves as individuals. We are, on the contrary, to seek to know man in and for himself ; and when we do so know him, we find that he is essentially social, and that the individual, as such, is a mere " fiction of the metaphysicians." Here again, therefore, we find that Comte's system ends in a compromise between opposite tendencies of thought. As his subjective synthesis after all was found to be objective, at least so far as mankind were concerned, so in like manner his opposition of the intellect to the heart turns out to be only partial ; for when the intelligence is directed to psychology and sociology, it gives us an idea of humanity, according to which all men are " members one of another." The warfare of the heart and the intelligence thus resolves itself into another expression of that dualism between the world and man, which we have already considered.

The second question—whether the altruistic affections of man do not imply, or are not necessarily connected with, the development of his reason or self-consciousness—is even more important. Comte, like Hume, took all the desires, higher and lower, as tendencies given apart from the reason, which can only devise the means of satisfying them, and is, therefore, necessarily their servant. Reason itself on this view does not essentially affect the character of those tendencies which it obeys. "*Cupiditas est appetitus cum ejusdem conscientia,*" says Spinoza, and immediately he goes on to speak as if the "*conscientia*" made no change in the character of the "*appetitus.*" But if we think of appetites or desires—some of them tending to the good of the individual, others to the good of the species—as existing in an animal which is not conscious of a self, these appetites will neither be selfish nor unselfish in the sense in which we apply these terms to man. Where there is no *ego* there can be no *alter ego,* and therefore neither egoism nor altruism. The con-

Are not the social affections determined by reason?

sciousness of the self as a permanent unity to which all the different tendencies are referred, and the consequent rise of a new desire for the good or happiness, as distinct from the desires of particular objects, are essential to egoism.   The consciousness of an *alter ego, i.e.,* of a community with others which makes their interests our own, and hence the consequent rise of a love for them,—which is not disinterested merely as the animal appetites are disinterested, because they tend directly to their objects without any thought of self, but disinterested in the sense that the thought of self is conquered or transcended,—is essential to altruism. Each of these tendencies may coincide in its *matter*, or rather in its first matter, with the appetites ; viewed from the outside, they may seem to be nothing higher than hunger or thirst, and sexual or parental impulse; but their *form* is different.   In becoming combined with self-consciousness, they are changed as by a chemical solvent, which dissolves and renews them ; nay, as by a new principle of life, whose first transformation of them is nothing but the beginning of a series of transformations both of their matter and their form ; so that, in the end, the simple direct tendency to an object—the uneasiness which sought its cure without reflection either upon itself or upon anything else—is transmuted, on the one side, into a gigantic ambition and greed, which would make the whole world tributary to the lust of the individual, and, on the other side, into a love of humanity in which self-love is altogether transcended or absorbed. Neither of these, however, nor any lower form of either is in such wise *external* to reason, that we can talk of them as determining it to an end which is not its own. Both are simply the expression in feeling of that essential opposition of the self to the not-self, and at the same time that essential unity of the self with the not-self, which are the two opposite, but complementary, aspects of the life of reason. And the progressive triumph of altruism over egoism, which constitutes the moral significance of history, is only the result of the fact that an individual, who is also a conscious self, cannot find his happiness in his own individual life, but only in the life of the whole to which he belongs. A selfish life is for such a being a contradiction. It is a life in which he is at war with himself as well as with others, for it is the life of a being who,

though essentially social, tries to find satisfaction
in a personal or individual good.   His "intelligence " and his " heart " equally condemn such a
life ; it is not only a crime but a blunder.   For a
spiritual being, as such, is one who can save his
life only by losing it in a wider life, one who must
die to himself in order that he may live.   In the
progress of man's spirit, therefore, there is no
necessary or possible schism between the two
parts of his being ; but, on the contrary, the
development of the one implies the development of the other.   It is the more comprehensive
idea, as well as the higher social purpose, which
always triumphs ; and if what is called intellectual culture sometimes seems to have the worse
in the struggle for existence, it is because it is a
superficial or formal culture, which does not really
represent the most comprehensive idea.

Bearing of
this opposi-
tion on
Comte's
view of
history.

This leads us to observe that the opposition of
the heart to the intelligence is Comte's key to
the whole history of the past, especially in relation to religion.   Theology is to him a system
growing out of a natural, though partially errone-
ous, hypothesis, an hypothesis which in its first
appearance was well suited to excite the nascent

intelligence and satisfy the primary affections of man, but which, in its further development, tended to secure moral and social ends at the 'expense of truth, and became more and more irrational as it became more and more useful. Fetichism, the first religion, was the spontaneous result of man's primitive tendency to exaggerate the likeness of all things to himself. It is "less distant from Positivity" than any other sort of theology,* for its only error is that it supposes the existence of life wherever it finds activity, an error which can "easily be brought to the test of verification" and corrected. "We can show it to be an error, and so get rid of it." But Polytheism, seeking for greater generality, refers phenomena, not directly, to beings who are identified with them, but indirectly, to "wills belonging to beings purely imaginary," whose "existence can no more be decisively disproved than it can be demonstrated." Further, Polytheism extends to the order of man's life that kind of explanation which Fetichism necessarily confined to nature, because the latter sought to explain everything by man, and

* Pol. Pos. iii. p. 85 : Trans. p. 71.

never thought of man himself as requiring explanation. But this, while it has the advantage of bringing human life within the domain of speculation, at the same time reduces theology into a palpable instance of reasoning in a circle. For "humanity cannot legitimately be included in the synthesis of causes, from the very fact that its type is found in man." * Last of all comes Monotheism, concentrating still further the theological explanation of the universe, but rendering it still more incoherent and irrational, for "the conception of a single God involves a type of absolute perfection complete in each of the three aspects of human nature, affection, thought, and action. Now, such a conception unavoidably contradicts itself, for either this all-powerful Being must be inferior to ourselves, morally or intellectually, or else the world which he created must be free from those radical imperfections which, in spite of Monotheistic sophistry, have been always but too evident. And even were this second alternative admissible, there would remain a yet deeper inconsistency. Man's moral and mental faculties have for their object to sub-

* Pol. Pos. iii. p. 261 : Trans. p. 218.

serve practical necessities, but an omnipotent Being can have no occasion either for wisdom or for goodness." *

What reconciles mankind, and especially the men of light and leading, to these intellectually un-satisfactory conceptions of God, is their practical value in extending and strengthening the social bond.   Polytheism was superior to Fetichism, because it lent itself to the formation of that wider community, which we call the State, whereas Fetichism tended rather to confine the sympathies of men to the narrower limits of the family.   And Monotheism was the neces-sary basis of that still wider society which binds men to each other simply as men, and apart from any special ties of blood or language.   This at least was the case so long as the truth of the unity of humanity had not yet assumed a scien-tific form, and therefore still needed an external support.   But when the sciences of sociology and morals arise, this external scaffolding ceases to be necessary, and must even become injurious, as, indeed, Theology at the best is ill-adapted to the social end it has been made to subserve.

Monotheism the great instrument of social unity.

* Ibid. iii. p. 431 : Trans. p. 365.

Though, in itself, it is radically unsocial.

This last point deserves special attention. According to Comte, Theology, and above all, Monotheistic Theology, is a system the direct influence of which is altogether unfavourable to the social tendencies, although indirectly, by the course of history, and through the wise modifications to which it has been subjected by the leaders and teachers of mankind, it has become the main instrument in developing altruism. The increasing generality of theological belief, indeed, was a necessary condition of the establishment of social unity; but, by directing the eyes of men not to themselves but to supernatural beings, by making the issues of life turn on the favour or disfavour of such beings rather than on the social action and reaction of men upon each other, and by reducing this world into a secondary position, and subordinating its concerns to those of another world, Theology tended to dissolve rather than to knit closer the bonds of society. The relation of the individual to God isolated him from his fellows. Especially was this the case with the Christian form of Monotheism, with its tremendous future rewards and penalties, and the direct relation which it established between the soul of the individual and the infinite Being. "The immediate effect of putting personal salvation in the foremost place was to create an unparalleled selfishness, a selfishness rendering all social influences nugatory, and thus tending to dissolve public life." * "The Christian type of life was never fully realized except by the hermits of the Thebaid," who, "by narrowing their wants to the lowest standard, were able to concentrate their thoughts without remorse or distraction on the attainment of salvation." † What else, indeed, but egoism could be awakened by the worship of a God who is himself the supreme type of egoism? For "the desires of an omnipotent Being, being gratified as soon as formed, can consist in nothing but pure caprices. There can be no appreciable motive either from within or from without. And above all, these pure caprices must of necessity be purely personal; so that the metaphysical formula, *To live in self for self*, would be alike applicable to the two extreme grades of the vital scale. The type of divinity thus approximates to the lowest stage

* Pol. Pos. iii. p. 411: Trans. p. 348.
† Ibid. iii. p. 454: Trans. p. 383.

O

of animality, the only shape in which life is purely individual, because it is reduced to the one function of nutrition." *   The natural result of such a religion was, therefore, to discourage the altruistic affections: as, indeed, Monotheism has systematically denied that such affections form part of the nature of man.

How its un-social char-acter was neutralized.   The alchemy which, according to Comte, turned this poison into wholesome food, was found in the altruistic affections of the teachers of mankind, which led them to limit and modify the doctrine they taught, so as to subserve man's moral improvement.   This, however, would not have been sufficient, if these teachers had not at an early period ceased to be a theocracy, or, in other words, if the practical government of mankind had not been wrested from their hand by the military classes.   By this change, which contained in itself the germ of the separation of the Church from the State, of theory from practice, of counsel from command, the priests, prophets, or philosophers, who were the intellectual leaders of men, were reduced to that position of subordination in which alone

* Ibid. iii. p. 446: Trans. p. 376.

they can concentrate their attention upon their proper work. For the influences of the intellect, like those of the affections, must be indirect if they are to be pure. "No power, especially if it be theological, cares to modify the will, unless it finds itself powerless to control action." But when the theoretic class were subordinated to the practical class, they became the natural allies of the women, and, like them, had to substitute counsel for command. At first, indeed, their subjection was too absolute, for the military aristocracies of Greece and Rome did not leave to the priesthood sufficient independence, or at least sufficient authority, to permit even of counsel. But with the rise of Catholic Mono- theism, supported as it was by a new revelation based upon the idea of an incarnation of God, the separation of Church and State was definitely established, and the intellectual life was put in its proper relation to the life of action.

The consequence is that the theological priest- How Chris- hood have continually sought to counteract the tian Mono- theism was natural influences of their doctrine by mak- humanized. ing additions which were inconsistent with its "absolute" principle, but which rendered it better fitted for the purpose of binding men together. This was especially the 'case under Monotheism, where, as we have seen, such counteraction was most necessary. From this source arose a series of supplementary doctrines, generally tending to connect God with man, and men with each other. St. Paul, "the real founder of Catholicism," took the first step in reducing Monotheism into a shape in which it could act as an "organic" doctrine; and his successors followed steadily in the same path. If the omnipotence of God raised Him above all human sympathy, and tended to destroy human sympathy in his worshippers, the doctrines of the Trinity and the Incarnation again brought God near to men, and taught them to reverence in themselves a humanity which was raised into unity with God. In the Feast of the Eucharist all men celebrated and enjoyed their unity with this exalted and deified humanity. The same influence, in its further development, led to the adoration of the saints, and above all of the Virgin Mother, in whom Christian devotion really worshipped Humanity, in its simplest and tenderest affections. Finally, if benevolent sympathies were denied to nature, St. Paul found a place for them by attri-

buting them to grace, " which Thomas à Kempis
admirably defines as the equivalent of love—
gratia sive dilectio—divine inspiration being substituted for human impulse."* And the struggle
between egoism and altruism was expressed in the
doctrines of the Fall and Redemption of mankind.†
Thus the social passion which, according to the
theory, could not be derived from human nature,
was conceived to flow from a divine influence,
and became ennobled, at least as a means of salvation, in the eyes of those who would otherwise
have suppressed it. At the same time, as Comte
also contends, these additions or corrections of the
original doctrine were inconsistent or imperfect in
themselves, and inadequate to the social purpose
for which they were destined; and they naturally
disappeared whenever, by the emancipation of the
intelligence, the immense egoism, which Monotheism consecrated in God and favoured in man,
was let loose from the bonds in which the Church
had confined it. Protestantism was the first indication of this change; for Protestantism is but
an organized anarchy, and the only elements of

* Pol. Pos. iii. p. 447 : Trans. p. 378.
† Ibid. iii. p. 409 : Trans. 346.

order in it are derived from an instinctive conservatism, clinging to the fragments of a past doctrinal system which, in principle, has been abandoned. It contains no organic elements of its own—no positive contribution to the progressive life of humanity; it is simply the first imperfect result of that metaphysical individualism which, in its ultimate form, freed from all the limits of the Catholic system, expressed itself theoretically in Rousseau and Voltaire, and practically in the French Revolution. The hope of mankind, however, lies in the new synthesis of Positivism, which alone can give due value to the innate altruistic sympathies of man; for it alone can place on a permanent scientific basis that social order which the mediæval Church attempted in vain to found on the essentially egoistic and anarchic doctrine of Monotheism.

Opposition of elements in the religions of the past.

The fundamental conception, then, which underlies Comte's view of progress is, that every past religion, with the partial exception of Fetichism, has been an amalgam of two radically inconsistent elements, of which only one was due to the theological principle itself; while the other was due, partly to the practical instinct of its priests, which led them to modify the logical results of that principle in conformity with the social wants of man; and partly also to their subordinate position, which obliged them to use the spiritual means of conviction and persuasion instead of the ruder weapons of material force. To criticize this theory fully would be to re-write Comte's history of religion. It will be sufficient here to point out that his view of modern history begins in a false interpretation of Christianity, and ends in an equally false interpretation of the Protestant Reformation.

Christianity from its origin has two aspects or elements; and if we compare it with earlier religions, we may call these its Pantheistic and its Monotheistic elements. But these elements are not, as Comte asserts, joined together by a mere external necessity. They are necessarily connected in the inner logic of the system; nor can we regard one of them as more or less essential than the other. In the simplest words of the Gospels we find already expressed a sense of reconciliation with God, and therefore with the world and self, which is alien to pure Monotheism, though there is some faint anticipation of

Did this discord exist in Christianity?

it in the later books of the Old Testament. For a spiritual Monotheism, while it awakens a consciousness of the holiness of God, and the sinfulness of the creature, tends to make fear prevail over love, and the sense of separation over the sense of union. The idea of the unity of the Divine and the Human—an original unity which yet has to be realized by self-sacrifice—and the corresponding idea that the individual or natural life must be lost in order to save it, were presented for the first time, as in one great living picture, in the life and death of Christ. And what was thus directly presented to the heart and the imagination in an individual, was universalized in the writings of St. Paul and St. John; in other words, it was there liberated from its peculiar national setting, and used as a key to the general moral history of man. The Messiah of the Jews was exalted into the Divine Logos, and the Cross became the symbol of an atonement and reconciliation between God and man, which has been made "before the foundation of the world," yet which has to be made again in every human life. The work of the first three centuries was to give to this idea such logical expression as was then possible, in the doctrines of the Incarnation and the Trinity. It is true that this idea of the unity of man with God was not immediately carried out to any of the consequences which might seem to be contained in it. It remained for a time a religion, and a religion only; it did not show itself to be the principle of a new social or political order of life. Rather it accepted the old order represented by the Roman Empire, and even consecrated it as "ordained of God," only demanding for itself that it should be allowed to purify the inner life of men. Such a separation of the things of Cæsar and the things of God was then inevitable; for it is impossible that a new principle can ever be received simply and without alloy into minds, which are at the same time occupying themselves with its utmost practical or even its utmost theoretical consequences. In this sense there is much truth in what Comte says about the value of the separation of the spiritual from the temporal authority. The power of directly realizing a new religious principle, just because it draws away attention from the principle itself to the details of its practical application, is likely to prevent that application being either a complete or even a true expression of the principle. Practical inferences from such a principle cannot safely be drawn by mere logical deduction; they will be drawn with certainty and effect only by those whose whole spiritual life the principle has remoulded. The decided withdrawal of the Christian Church from the sphere of " practical politics " was, therefore, not merely a necessity forced upon it from without; it was a condition which its best members gladly accepted, because without it the inner transformation of man's life by the new doctrine would have been impossible. If Christianity had raised a servile insurrection it never could have put an end to slavery.

Growth of dualism in the middle ages.

But while this withdrawal was necessary, it contained a great danger; for the inner life cannot be separated from the outer life without becoming narrowed and distorted. Confined to the sphere of religion and private morality, the doctrine of unity and reconciliation necessarily became itself the source of a new dualism. What had been at first merely neglect of the world was gradually changed into hostility to worldly interests; and the germs of a positive morality, reconciling the flesh and the spirit, which appear in the New Testament, were neglected and over-shadowed in the growth of asceticism. Chris-tianity, even in its first expression, had a negative side towards the natural life of man; while it lifted man to God, it yet taught that humanity " cannot be quickened except it die." But the mediæval Church, while it constantly taught that humanity must die to all its natural impulses, had almost forgotten to hope that it could be quickened. Its highest morality—the morality of the three vows—was the negation of all social obligations; its science was the interpretation of a fixed dogma received on authority; its religion tended to become an external service, an *opus operatum*, a preparation for another world, rather than a principle of action in this. Its highest act of worship, the Eucharist, in which was celebrated the revealed unity of men with each other and with God, was reserved in its fulness for the clergy, and even with them was finally reduced to an external act by the doctrine of tran-substantiation, in which poetry " became logic," and in becoming logic, ceased to be truth.

Now, Comte, seeing the working of this Unity of the two elements in Chris-tianity.

negative tendency in mediæval Catholicism, and regarding it as the natural work of Monotheism, is obliged to treat all the positive side of Christianity as an external addition suggested by the practical wisdom of the clergy. St. Paul is supposed by him to have invented (and Comte's language would even suggest that he consciously invented*) the doctrine of grace, in order to reconsecrate those social affections which Monotheism, in its condemnation of nature, had either denied to exist, or, what is nearer the truth, had treated as having no moral value. But this only shows how imperfectly Comte had grasped the Pauline conception of the moral change which religion produces. The idea that the immediate untamed and undisciplined will of the natural man is not a principle of morality, and that therefore man must die to live, must rise above himself to be himself, is one which has in it nothing discordant with the claims of social feeling. It is the commonplace of every powerful writer on practical ethics, from the Gospels to Thomas à Kempis, and from Luther to Goethe.

---

* Pol. Pos. iii. p. 409 : Trans. p. 346.

" Und so lang du das nicht hast,
   Dieses : Stirb und Werde,
   Bist du nur ein trüber Gast
   Auf der dunkeln Erde."

St. Paul adds that this death to self is possible only to him in whom another than his own natural will lives; "so then it is not I that live, but Christ that liveth in me." Comte would accept the words of St. Paul with the substitution of Humanity for Christ. But either substitution involves the negation of the natural tendencies, whether individual or social, in their immediate natural form ; and Comte himself, when he placed not only the sexual but even the maternal impulse among those that are merely " personal or egoistic," virtually acknowledged that the natural or instructive basis of the altruistic affections is not in itself moral.* But because he begins with a psychology which treats the egoistic and altruistic desires, and again the intellect and the heart, as distinct and independent entities, he is unable to do justice to an account of moral experience which involves that they are essentially related elements

* Ibid. i. p. 726: Trans. p. 562.

in one whole, or necessarily connected stages of its development.

Their opposition in its development.

In the form in which it was first presented, the teaching of Christianity was undoubtedly ambiguous, as, indeed, every doctrine in its first and simplest form must be. In that form we cannot, without limitations, call it either social or anti-social; it is anti-social and ascetic, because of its negative relations to the previous forms of life and culture; it is social and positive, in so far as in its primary doctrine of the unity of the divine and human—of divinity manifested in man and humanity made perfect through suffering—it contains the promise and the necessity of a development by which nature and spirit shall be reconciled. The progressive tendency of Christendom was based on the fact that from the earliest times the followers of Christ were placed in the dilemma, either of denying their primary doctrine of reconciliation between God and man and going back to pure Monotheism, or of advancing to the reconciliation of all those other antagonisms of spirit and nature, the world and the Church, which arose out of the circumstances of its first publication. And modern history is more than anything else the history of the long process whereby this logical necessity manifested itself in fact. The negative spirit of the Middle Age, its asceticism, its dualism, its formalism, its tendency to transform the moral opposition of natural and spiritual into an external opposition between two separate worlds, present and future, and thus to substitute " other-wordliness " for worldliness, instead of substituting unworldliness for both—all these characteristics were the natural results of the fact that the idea of Christianity, in its first abstract form, could not include, and therefore necessarily became opposed to, the forms of social life and organization with which it came into contact. But while the early Christians looked for the realization of the kingdom of Heaven in some immediate earthly future, and the Middle Age postponed it to another life, Christ had already taught the truth, which alone can turn either of these hopes into something more than the expression of an egoistic desire—the truth that " the kingdom of God is within us." The reaction of the social necessities of mediæval society on the doctrine—which Comte quite correctly describes as leading to the

gradual elevation of humanity and of human
interests—found its main support in the principles of the doctrine itself, so soon as its lessons
had been absorbed into the mind of the people.
And the irresistible force of the movement,
whereby at a later period the intelligence was
emancipated from authority, and the claims
of the family and the State were asserted
against the Church, lay above all in this, that
Christianity itself was felt to involve the
consecration of human life in all its interests
and relations. Luther's appeal to the New
Testament and to the earliest ages of Christianity was in some ways unhistorical, but it
expressed a truth. Protestantism was not a
return to the Christianity of the first century; it
was an assertion of the relation of the individual
to God, which was itself made possible only by
the long work of Latin Catholicism. But the
development of a doctrine, if it has in it any
germ of truth which is capable of development,
involves a continual recurrence to its first, and
therefore its most general, expression. The elements successively developed in the Catholic
and the Protestant, the Latin and the Germanic

forms of Christianity, were both present in the original germ, and the exaggerated prominence given in the former to the *negative* side of Christianity could not but lead, in the development of thought, to a similarly exaggerated manifestation of its *positive* side. But it is nearly as absurd to say, as Comte does, that the true logical outcome of Christianity is to be found in the "life of the hermits of the Thebaid," as it would be to say that its true logical outcome is to be found in those vehement assertions of nature—naked and unashamed—as its own sufficient warrant, which poured almost with the force of inspiration from the lips of Diderot. ' Both extremes are equally removed from that special moral temper and tone of feeling which we call distinctively Christian—the former by its want of sympathy and tenderness, no less than the latter by its want of purity and self-command. Reassertion of nature through its negation, or to put it more simply, the purification of the natural desires by the renunciation of their immediate gratification, is the idea that is more or less definitely present in all phases of the history of Christianity; and, though swaying from one side to the other, the religious life of modern times has never ceased to present both aspects.   Even a St. Augustine recoiled from the Manichæism by which nature was regarded, not simply as fallen from its original idea, but as essentially impure.   And, on the other hand, even Rousseau's Savoyard vicar, who freed himself from the negative or ascetic element as completely as is possible for any one still retaining any tincture of Christianity or even of religion, and who insists so strongly on the text that "the natural is the moral," is yet forced to recognize that nature has two voices, and that the *raison commune* has to overcome and transform the natural inclinations of the individual.   In the life of its Founder, the Christian Church has always had before it an individual type of that harmony of the spiritual and natural life, which it is its ideal to realize in all the wider social relations of man; nor, till that ideal is reached, can it be said that the Christian idea is exhausted, or that the place is vacant for a new religion,—great as may be the changes of form and expression through which Christianity must pass under the changed conditions of modern life.

That Comte was not able to discern this, arose, as we have seen, from the fact that he held to a kind of Manichæism of his own. To him the egoistic and the altruistic desires were two kinds of innate tendencies, both of which exist in man from the first, though with a great preponderance on the side of egoism.* Moral improvement

---

* Comte insists with great force on the danger of taking an organism as the mere sum of its parts, or its life as merely the resultant of their external action and reaction upon each other: but in his psychological analysis, he often seems to forget this principle. If he recognizes that, as we rise in the scale of animal life, there is a continually advancing differentiation of the simple unity we find in the lowest organisms, he does not always remember that this implies and necessitates a correspondent integration. Hence in the end the unity which he establishes between the different elements, *e.g.*, between the intellect and the heart, or between the egoistic and the social impulses, is external and artificial. In his Psychology the fact that it is *I* who think, *I* who feel, *I* who desire finds no sufficient place, and, therefore, in his Ethics he can reach no ideal except that of an external harmony of the different faculties and tendencies. Where the *primary* unity below the difference and conflict of the parts is not recognized, it becomes impossible to see beyond their antagonism to its reconciliation in a *final* unity.

See especially Comte's sketch of Psychology in the third chapter of the *Introduction Fondamentale*. Pol. Pos. i. 685, *seq.*

simply consists in altering the original proportions in favour of altruism, and moral perfection would be the complete extinction of egoism (which with Comte would naturally mean the extinction of all the desires classified as personal). Hence there is a somewhat ascetic tendency in some of the ideas of the *Politique Positive*—*i.e.*, asceticism sometimes appears in it, not simply as a transitionary process through which certain natural desires are to be purified, but as an attempt, so far as possible, to extinguish them. A deeper analysis would have shown that the desires in themselves, as mere natural impulses, are neither egoistic nor altruistic, neither bad nor good ; and that if, as they appear in the self-conscious life of men, they are necessarily infected with egoism, yet that the *ego* is not absolutely opposed to the *alter ego*, but rather implies it. A spiritual or self-conscious being is one who can realize his own individual good only as he realizes the good of others: but, in seeking to realize such a good, it is not needful that he should renounce any natural desire as impure; for there is no natural desire which may not become the expression of the better self, which is *ego* and *alter ego* in one.

But Comte, unable from the limitations of his
psychology to see the true relation of the negative
and the positive side of ethics, is obliged to treat
the ascetic tendency of Christianity as involving
a denial of the existence in man of innate social
sympathies; and on the other hand, to regard the
efforts of the Christian Church to cultivate such
sympathies, as the result of an external accom-
modation. His idea of Christianity practically
coincides with the definition of virtue given by
Paley; it is " doing good to man, in obedience to
the will of God, with a view to eternal happiness." On this view the Christian life is the
pursuit of a selfish end by means in themselves
unselfish, or it is selfishness turned to unselfish
action in view of the pleasures and pains of another
world ; and so soon as doubt is cast upon these
supernatural rewards and punishments, the false
show of benevolence must disappear and leave
bare selfishness in its place. Hence Comte is just
neither to Catholicism nor to Protestantism ; for,
while he maintains the former to be only *indirectly* social, he regards the latter as the first
step in a scepticism which, taking away the fears
and hopes of another world, must at the same

time take away all restraint upon selfishness. And, just because he is unable fully to understand either the negative spirit of the earlier, or the positive spirit of the later, phase of modern life, he has an imperfect appreciation of that social ideal to which both are tending, and which must combine in itself the true elements of both. Yet we cannot say that he is equally unfair to Catholicism and to Protestantism. It is the temptation of writers on social subjects to be least just to the tendencies of the time which precedes their own, and against the errors of which they have immediately to contend. Hence we are not surprised to find that Comte does more justice to Catholicism than to Protestantism, or to that Individualism which grew out of Protestantism. The Reformation and what is called in German the *Aufklärung* he regards solely on their destructive side, as successive stages in the modern movement of revolt, while he fails to appreciate the constructive elements involved in each of them. Hence also, in his attitude towards this great movement, he all but identifies himself with Catholic writers like De Maistre; and his own scheme of the future is essentially reactionary.

The restoration of the spiritual power to its mediæval position was for Comte a natural proposal, because he could see in the Protestant revolt nothing more than an insurrectionary movement, which might clear the way for a new social construction, but which in itself was the negation of all government whatever.

But what was Protestantism ? To the Protestant it seemed to be simply a return to the original purity of the Christian faith; to the Catholic, it seemed to be a fatal revolt against the only organization by which Christianity could be realized. Really it partook of both characters. It involved a dangerous misconception of the social conditions, under which alone the religious life can be realized and developed ; but it involved also a deeper and truer apprehension of that religion, which first recognized the latent divinity, or universal capacity, of every spiritual being as such, and, which, therefore, seemed to impose upon every individual man the right or rather the duty of living by the witness of his own spirit. Comte saw only the former of these two aspects of it. Hence he regarded the French Revolution as a practical refutation of the individ-

The defects of Protestantism.

ualism which grew out of the Protestant movement, and not, as it was in truth, a critical
event, which forced men to distinguish and
separate its true from its false elements.   He
drew from it, indeed, a true lesson—the lesson
that the individual as such has no moral or
religious life of his own, and that it is only
in proportion as he transcends his own individuality and lives in the life of humanity, that
his spiritual life can have any depth or riches
in it.   "We are afraid to put men to live
and trade each on his own private stock
of reason, because we suspect that the stock in
each man is small, and that the individuals
would do better to avail themselves of the
general bank and capital of nations and of ages."
The truth expressed in these words was seen as
clearly by Comte as by Burke.   And because
he saw it, Comte regarded the Protestant Individualism, which throws individuals back upon
themselves, as tending merely to empty their
minds of all real interests, and to deliver
them over to their own caprices.   Private
judgment and popular government were to him
only pretentious names for intellectual and

political anarchy; and his remedy for the
moral diseases of modern times was the restoration of that division of the spiritual and
temporal authorities, which existed in the Middle
Ages.

There is, however, another aspect of the The good side of Protestant-ism.
Protestantism and of the apparently anarchical
doctrines derived from it, to which Comte pays
no attention. Catholicism, as we have seen,
had developed one aspect of Christianity, until,
by its exclusive prominence, the principle of
Christianity itself was on the point of being
lost. It had changed the division between laity
and clergy, world and Church, from a relative to
an absolute division; it had presented Christian
doctrine, not as something which the spirit of
the individual may ultimately verify for itself,
but as something which it must submissively
accept without any verification. It had made
Christian worship into an *opus operatum,* a
work done by the priest for the people, instead
of a means through which the feelings of the
people could be at once drawn out and expressed. Now, it is as opposed to these tendencies that the Protestant movement had its

highest value. Each of the so-called anarchic doctrines, against which Comte protests,
has a good as well as a bad meaning. If, *e.g.*,
it is nothing less than intellectual anarchy
for every individual to claim to judge for
himself, on subjects for which he has not
the requisite training or discipline, it is a
slavery scarcely less corrupting in its effect
than anarchy, when he is made to regard
the difference between himself and his teachers
as a permanent and absolute one. In the
former case, he has no sufficient feeling of his
want to make him duly submissive to teaching; in the latter, he has no sufficient consciousness of his capacity to be taught, to permit a
due reaction of his thought upon the matter
received from his teachers. Again, the doctrine
of the sovereignty of the people is the negation
of all government and social order, if it be
taken to mean that the uninstructed many should
govern themselves by their own insight, and
that the instructed few should simply be their
servants and their instruments. But where the
people are not recognized as the ultimate source
of power, where their consent is not in any

regular way made necessary to the proceedings of
their governors, they are by that very fact kept
in a perpetual tutelage, and cannot possibly feel
that the life of the state is their own life. Now,
the most important effect of the Protestant movement was just this, that it awakened in the
individual the consciousness of his universal
nature, or, in other words, the consciousness that
there is no external power or sovereignty, divine
or human, to which he has absolutely and per-
manently to submit, but that every outward
claim of authority must ultimately be justified by
the inner witness of his own spirit. The freedom
of man consists in this, that his obedience to the
State, to the Church, even to God, is the obedience of his natural to his spiritual self. The
essential truth of the Reformation lay in its
republication of the doctrine that the voice of God
speaks not only without but also within us, and
indeed that " it is only by the God within that
we can comprehend the God without." And the
nations, which had learned that lesson in religion,
soon hastened to apply it to the social and
political order of life. It is undoubtedly a
lesson which is liable to misapprehension, as

may be seen, not only from the tendency of many Protestant sects to put the inner life in opposition to the outer, and so to deprive the former of all wider contents and interests ; but also from the ultimate substitution, by Rousseau and others, of the assertion of the natural, for the assertion of the spiritual, man. By such writers the mere *capacity* of man for a higher life is treated as if it were the higher life itself : and it is forgotten that the capacity is nothing unless it be realized, and that its realization requires the surrender of individual liberty and private judgment to the guidance and teaching of those, in whom that realization has already taken place. But it is not the less true that the consciousness of the capacity, and consequently of the duty, of becoming not merely a slave or instrument, but an organ, of the intellectual and moral life of mankind, is the essential basis of modern life. " Henceforth, I call ye not servants, for the servant knoweth not what his lord doeth ; but I have called you friends," is a word of Christ which scarcely began to be verified till the Reformation. And while its verification cannot mean the negation of that division of labour upon which society rests,—cannot mean that each one should *know* and *judge*, any more than that each one should *do*, everything for himself, —it at least means that every power and authority should henceforth be, in the true sense of the word, a spiritual power, and should, therefore, rest for its main support upon the opinion of those who obey it. It is because he has not appreciated this truth that Comte so decidedly breaks with the democratic spirit of modern times, and seeks to set up an aristocracy in the State and a monarchy in the Church. Yet the spirit of the age is, after all, too strong for him, and while he refuses to the governed any regular and legitimate way of reacting upon the powers that govern them, he recognizes that the *ultima ratio*, the final remedy for misgovernment, lies in their irregular and illegitimate action. As regards the State, he declares that " the right of insurrection is the ultimate resource with which no society should allow itself to dispense." * And as regards the Church he says that if " the High Priest of Humanity, supported by the body of the clergy, should go

* Cf. Pol. Pos. i. 128 *seq.*

wrong, then the only remedy left would be the refusal of co-operation, a remedy which can never fail, as the priesthood rests solely on conscience and opinion, and succumbs, therefore, to their adverse sentence." The civil government, in fact, can bring the spiritual power to a dead-lock, by " suspending its stipend, for in cases of serious error popular subscriptions would not replace it, unless on the supposition of a fanaticism scarcely compatible with the Positive faith, where there is enthusiasm for the doctrines, rather than for the teachers."* Comte also desiderates a strong reactive influence of public opinion from the proletariate, by which the officers, both of Church and State, may be kept faithful to their work. But if this is desirable, why should the proletariate have no regular means of making their will felt ? An "organic" theory of the constitution of society must surely provide every real force with a legitimate form of expression ; if a social theory embodies the idea of revolution in it, it is self-condemned.

Comte's partial revival of the mediæval system.

Comte's social ideal is in many respects a close reproduction of the mediæval system, with its

* Pol. Pos. iv. 337: Trans. 294.

régime dispersif of feudalism in the world, and its Papal concentration of authority in the church. For him, the establishment of the national State is as great an error in secular politics, as is the increasing division of labour in the spiritual kingdom of science. Still more strongly, if possible, does he reprobate that mingling of the functions of Church and State, that interference of the secular authority with spiritual matters, such as the education of the people and its religious life, which has been the natural consequence of the failure of the mediæval Church to maintain its old authority. Notwithstanding his worship of Humanity, the idea of a "parliament of man, a federation of the world," by which all the powers of mankind should be united for the attainment of the highest material and spiritual good, has no attraction for him. To reduce the State to the dimensions of a commune, and to confine it to the care of purely material interests, is his first political proposal. France, England, and Spain (and we may now add Germany and Italy) are, in his view, "factitious aggregates without solid justification," and they will only become "free and durable States," when they are broken up into fragments, each with a population of two or three millions, and a territory not exceeding that of Belgium or Tuscany. The "West" will thus be divided into seventy republics, and the earth into five hundred; and the main work of the patriciate will be to direct and regulate the industrial life of the community: each member of the banker triumvirate, who are to be at the head of the State, having one of the great industrial departments under his special superintendence. On the other hand the unity of humanity is to be represented solely by the spiritual power, in whose hands is to be left the whole work of advancing science, teaching the people, and exercising a moral censorship over all Governments and individuals. And while this spiritual power is, for practical purposes, to be strictly organized on the model of the mediæval Church, it is also, like that Church, to remain, for scientific purposes, inorganic. In other words, it is to admit no division of labour in science, but every scientific man, like a mediæval doctor, is to profess all science, adding to this the priestly office, which, with Comte, includes both the cure of souls and of bodies.

To criticize the details of this scheme seems to be unnecessary after what has been already said. It is not to be denied that the division of Church and State in the Middle Ages was a most important and even a necessary condition of progress. Christianity could never have been impressed upon the minds of men, if the concrete application of its principles had been too rapid. The essential condition of such application was that men should not concern themselves too prematurely with it. For the consequences of a moral and religious principle cannot be reached by direct logical deduction; it is like a living germ, in which, by no analysis or dissection, you can discover the lineaments of the future plant. To find out what it really is, or involves, you must plant it in the minds of men, and let it grow. Hence the mediæval Church was strong in its weakness, and it was its very victories over the temporal power that were its greatest danger. It became corrupt and lost its hold upon the minds of men, just when it seemed to have established its right to an absolute supremacy. Comte, following De Maistre, attaches great importance to the position of the Popes as arbiters between

Q

the Sovereigns and nations of mediæval Europe. But he forgets that in claiming and maintaining this position, the Popes were distinctly ceasing to be a spiritual power, if it be the function of a spiritual power to inculcate principles rather than to use them to solve practical difficulties. A power interfering in this way with the immediate struggle of interests could not but be invaded by the passions they excite, and it was the more certain to be corrupted by these passions, because it conceived them to be evil, and pretended altogether to renounce them. The authority acquired by the Church in the Middle Ages might have its value, as an anticipation of the peaceful federation of the nations under one supreme Government, but it was undoubtedly the first step towards the erasing of the distinction between the temporal and the spiritual power.

Their necessary conflict, when separated.

The truth seems to be that the distinction of secular and spiritual powers, except in the sense already indicated, is essentially irrational, and that the attempt to realize it in practice must involve, as it did involve in the Middle Ages, a continual internecine struggle. To set up two regularly constituted powers face to face with each other, one claiming man's allegiance in the name of his spiritual, and the other in the name of his temporal, interests, is to organize anarchy. So long as man's body and soul are inseparable, it will be impossible to divide the world between Cæsar and God; for in one point of view all is Cæsar's, and in another all is God's. In the Middle Ages the conflict of two despotisms was necessary to the growth of freedom; but, when government ceases to be despotic, the need for such division of power passes away. The relative separation between the speculative and the practical classes—between the scientific and moral teachers of mankind, who have to discover and inculcate principles, and the statesmen or administrators, who have to determine what improvements it is possible at a definite time to make in the organization of man's social and political life—is a division of labour which can surely be secured without breaking up the unity of the social body. It is not desirable that the philosopher, or priest, or man of science, should be king, (and we may even acknowledge that, if he were a king, he would probably be a very bad one): on the other hand, it *is* desirable that he should have his due influence, as the teacher of those general truths out of which all practical improvement must ultimately spring. But the natural difference of the tastes and capacities of men should, in a well-organized State, be sufficient to secure due influence to those who are the natural representatives of man's spiritual interests (whether they be religious, philosophic, or scientific), without tempting them, from their proper task of discovering and teaching the truth, to the less appropriate work of determining how much of it comes within "the sphere of practical politics." Comte, indeed, by organizing them as an independent power apart from, and outside of, the State, would make such a perversion extremely probable. A hierarchy of priests under a despotic Pope would soon cease to be, in any sense, a spiritual power; it would degenerate just as the Papacy degenerated in the fourteenth century; and this would be only the more certain if, by the Comtist denunciation of specialism, the priests were prohibited, in their own peculiar sphere of scientific research, from any division of labour according to capacity. For by this prohibition their attention would be diverted from inquiries about the truth of their doctrines to their immediate practical application; not to mention that, in the case of all but a few comprehensive minds, the natural result would be an omniscient superficiality, which would be the enemy of all real culture. Deprived of its natural object as a scientific order, the Comtist Priesthood would inevitably throw itself, with all its energy, into the task of directly influencing the practical life of men; and, if Comte's political ideas were carried out, it would find itself in the presence of a number of communal States, none of them large enough to offer any effective resistance. Positivism must indeed alter human nature, if such a priesthood would not seek to make itself despotic, especially if it could wield such a formidable weapon as the Positivist excommunication is supposed to be.*

The truth is that Comte commits the same error which misled Montesquieu when he supposed that the great security of a free State lay in the separation of the legislative, executive, and judicial powers,—*i.e.*, in treating the different organs through which the common life

Comte's social ideal not really organic.

* Pol. Pos. iv. p. 292.

expresses itself as if they were independent organisms.   He forgot that if such a balance of power was realized, the effect must either be an equilibrium in which all movement would cease, or a struggle in which the unity of the State would be in danger of being lost.   The true security against the dangers involved, on the one hand, in the direct application of theory to practice, and, on the other hand, in the too great separation of practice from theory, must lie, not in giving them independent positions as spiritual and temporal powers, but in subordinating them to the organic unity of the whole society, whether it be communal, national, or universal.   And organic unity, though it does not mean any special form of government, means at least two things: in the first place, that each great class or interest should have for itself a definite organ, and should therefore be able to act on the whole body in a regular and constitutional manner, so as to show all its force without revolutionary violence; and, in the second place, that no class or interest should have such an independent position, as to exclude every legal or constitutional method of bringing it into due subor-

dination to the common good. But Comte, losing
his balance in his jealousy of the individualistic
and democratic movement of modern society, has
built up a social ideal, which fails in both these
points of views, and which, indeed, is a revival
of the inorganic structure of mediæval society.

It would not be fair to conclude these chapters, Comte's position as a
which have necessarily been devoted in great part philosopher.
to criticism and controversy, without expressing
a sense of the power and insight which are shown
in the works of Comte, especially in the *Politique
Positive.* Controversy itself, it must be remem-
bered, is a kind of homage; for, as Hegel says,
" It is only a great man that condemns us to the
task of explaining him." But if we can sometimes look down upon such men, it becomes us
to remember that we stand upon their shoulders.
Comte seems to me to occupy, as a writer, a position in some degree analogous to that of Kant.
He stands, or rather moves, between the old
world and the new, and is broken into inconsistency by the effort of transition. Like Kant,
he is embarrassed to the end by the ideas with
which he started, and of which he can never free
himself so as to make a new beginning. Comte,

indeed, had only a small portion of that power of speculative analysis which characterized his great predecessor, but he had much of his tenacity of thought, his power of continuous construction; he had the same conviction of the all-importance of morals, and the same determination to make all theoretic studies subordinate to the solution of the moral problem.   Also, partly because he lived at a later time, and in the midst of a society which was in the throes of a social revolution, and partly because of the keenness and strength of his own social sympathies, he gives us a kind of insight into the diseases and wants of modern society, which we could not expect from Kant, and which throws new light upon the ethical speculations of Kant's idealistic successors.   To believe that his system, as a whole, is inconsistent with itself, that his theory of historical progress is insufficient, and that his social ideal is imperfect, need not prevent us from recognizing that there are many valuable elements in his historical and social theories, and that no one who would study such subjects can afford to neglect them.   A mind of such power cannot treat any subject without throwing much light upon it, which is independent of his special system of thought, and, above all, without doing much to show what are the really important difficulties in it which need to be solved. And, especially in such subjects, to discover the right question is to be half-way to the answer. Further, as Comte himself somewhere says, it is an immense advantage in studying any complex subject to have before us a distinct and systematic attempt to explain it; for it is only by criticism upon criticism that we can expect to reach the truth, in which its different sides and aspects are brought to a unity.

END.

GLASGOW : ROBERT MACLEHOSE, PRINTER TO THE UNIVERSITY

www.ingramcontent.com/pod-product-compliance
Lightning Source LLC
Chambersburg PA
CBHW020051030726
47498CB00006B/1738